Romancing God

Romancing God

The Divine Love Affair

Romancing God
The Divine Love Affair

Manna
Book V—2011

Doris Wellington

Romancing God: the Divine Love Affair
Volume Five: Manna
© Doris Wellington 2007-2023
Dwelling Places, home of books and letters
By Doris Wellington

All Rights Reserved

Unless otherwise noted
Scripture references taken from
Authorized King James Version of the Bible, Public Domain

Library of Congress Control Number—

First US Paperback Printing, 2023
KDP Independent Publishing Platform

Available on Amazon.com
and other online and retail outlets

ISBN-13: 978-0998150710

Cover Design
Nancy Bookhart

Dedication

I dedicate this book to my mother, Hattie Vance Wellington, who was the first person I ever heard talking to God with fervency and passion—who taught me how to approach God in moaning and groaning that could only be uttered by the Holy Spirit; and then wait patiently for the Father of all grace to answer. It WORKS!

I honor you for what you gave me—earth life, unconditional love, nurture of soul, faith in God, freedom to dream, wings to fly, and the unbridled force of your determined resolve. This is your enduring legacy, which I don't take lightly.
.

You're home now...

Introduction

I am not a student of certain religious rituals that others may apply in their personal search for spirituality, meaningful existence, or their quest to know or dismiss God. I do not claim powers any higher than the gifts I have been given to apply in seeking and reasonably satisfying my search for God. However, I believe that my hungry searching for God has awakened God in the core of my being, and revealed God to me in ways I could have never imagined; thus, creating a relationship only obtainable through this divine love affair.

While others may doubt that God would concern himself with the everyday contemplations of those who are as inconsequential to the world as some believe themselves to be, I hold firmly to the belief that these are exactly the ones to whom God willingly manifests. Over years of God seeking, these visitations—ofttimes multi-layered and interlocked, have taken various forms: including, but not limited to thousands of dreams, visions, love letters, conversations, and other manifestations of supernatural or paranormal origin, some of which, I have introduced in the nine-book series: *Romancing God: The Divine Love Affair*.

Romancing God: The Divine Love Affair is the simplest rendering of my interactions with God in this divine affair. Herein are the revelations of human transparency in the worship of God—fear, anxiety, imperfections, anger, love, heartbreak, loneliness, sin, all of the human heart and emotions exposed in the presence of God. And, though these revelations can never resolve the God enigma that eludes all of us, they are for me the response to the faith I offer him in the worshipping art of words.

Romancing God does not propose any particular construct upon which these visitations are built, received, or understood—they are not patterns to be followed—they are purely the expressions of my love in the personal relationship I live in God through faith. For me, it is just that simple.

Book One

Transported

The wind glides low beneath my feet

So I can mount upon wings of eagles

Ascending from here to there

January 01, 2011

Do you pity your life
Because it's not theirs
Or do they pity theirs
Because theirs is not yours
Would you rather
Their kingdom or mine
Be judged by your credit score
Or your righteous stand
Would you rather the cattle
On a thousand hills
Or command demons
Their plots to yield
Will you rather the order of man
Or the order of God
Walk among the Kings of the earth
That time will upend

Do not compare yourself
With their generals of war

Be the Apostle General
My Spirit born
Yearn not the praise
That mortals seek
Rather the glory
The apostles claimed
At my feet

What kind of life
Did their surrender demand
Once they made the decision
Their souls to yield

Turning entire cities
And nations around
Challenging the laws
Of social renown
And systems of government
To which Satan bowed

They were feared
Hated
But rarely celebrated
Ostracized
Denied
But never intimidated

Holding no allegiance
To empires or crowns
Wearing loose the pomp
By which others are bound
Power
Politics
Prudence
Piety
Pride
Prejudices
Pleasures
Of society

So what do you want
What is it you crave
The freedom of an heir
Or the fetters of slaves
A name that demons hear
Then scatter
Or the fragile trappings
Of ordinary matters
This world is yours
To rule and reign

Prince of Peace
Priest
Prophet
And King
All live
Inside of you

None walk higher
Than your calling
The honor I bestow
Confounds them all
They're not to be envied
Or emulated
Don't bow to their coffers
Or chase their dreams
Let them find you
Without apology for power

Let them stand in awe
Of this...
Your amazing hour
One hundred-fold
One thousand times return

Owing no institution
Indebted to none
So don't pity your life
Let them pity theirs
You hold the keys
To their lack

Enviable
Your house of treasures
The depth of which
None can measure
Whose I ask
Should hold more value
The eternal kingdom
Or the temporal

January 4, 12:28AM

Few people know
Friend or foe
The depth of loneliness
That I have bore
The prolonged nights
Of isolation
Studying your life
No one knows
The price I've paid
To claim each victory

The repose of soul
The depth of spirit
The harvest of faith
And the salt of wisdom

No one knows
The sacrifice
Or trail of tears
To claim this life
I vow to live
Minute by minute
Folds into years

I shall not die
But I shall live
This experience to declare
The best of my days
Is the one I'm in
Not ever looking back

2011 is my year
The latter rain belongs to me
Profuse and overflowing
From the cistern of my being
No impoverished past
No potential future
Shall impede
The now that I am living

The prophetic decree
Proclaims my time
Enlarge your tent
Stretch forth your borders
Lengthen your cords
Strengthen your stakes
For you shall break forth
On the right
And the left

Fear not
My daughter
My beloved

This is the season
I've prepared you for
Take no counterfeits
Refuse mimics
Every imposter
And falsehood
Shall suddenly diminish

The truth you represent
Is an eternal offering
The purity of your heart
Will not be disloyal
I have you
In the palms of my hand

The cut of every incision

I've born the pain

Wait no longer
The battle is not yours
Every adversary
Take by force

Remember
No enemies

Stand between us
The greatness of your hour
You're yet to witness

Believe
Breathe in the freshness
The genesis of your day
Is just beginning
As redundant
As this word may seem
The harvest I promised
You are about to glean

Hold open your hands
Stretch wide your arms
Enlarge your territory
Secure your heart
None shall enter
Who has not been cleansed
With the hyssop of trials
And Holy oil

You were right to say
There is no time for error
No margin for mistakes
No room to wiggle
Just gird up your loins

Take the sword of your faith
Press onward
General
Your army waits

Your gear has been sanctified
Your weapon made sure
There is nothing left now
But simply to do it

Take no prisoners of war
To boost your spiritual power
Give only what is yours
Do not negotiate survival
No weapon
No witness
Or conspiracy
Of man
Has power against you
While you're in my hand

And no one
I say none
In this shift of your destiny
Has the power
Or permission
To stop your blessing
I've seen your heart
Bled dry with tears
And love for those
Who just don't care

I've seen how you've walked
Among the lonely alone
But never without
Holding on
Fitted like a garment
Tailored for the storm
Triumph in places
That have subdued the strong
Taking the fight
Where the valiant die
Shouting the victory
Before it's been won

My daughter
You anchor my hope
There are still those
Who will follow your voice
Take heed

Be keenly engaged
In the move of the Spirit
Day by day
Awake to expectation
Lie down to praise
Do not count your blessings
Or number your days

For they
Will be immeasurable
Lengthened by my word
No boundary raised
No protest to render

Just walk after my heart
Keep your head adorned
In righteousness speak
The rest I will perform

And the harvest of your days
Will be multiplied and enviable

Beautiful to the eye
Beholding of the grace
In you I did impart
Let the world behold
The daughter
I begot...

January 11, 2011
Have I come now to know
Or perhaps see
That the mystery bone
Between my front shoulders
Form what appears to me
A dove
What else
With all that I have bore
In abnormal physiology
That begs the question
Of whether or not
I'm alien or human
This must be it

Yes...
A dove extending its wings

Will answer my life curiosity
With of all things
Doves...
Etching and sketching them
On journal pages
And notes

Was this to be a message for me
Each time I stand before a mirror
That God
Imprinted upon my flesh
A reminder that
I am never alone

Such depth of love which
I cannot phantom

Wings extended from a body
Astounds those who inquire
Of this peculiar image

I can give no science
Or reasoning
Nothing concrete
To exegesis
As to why my body bears
Such curious
Contradictions

The piercing pain behind my eyes
Examined by ophthalmologist
Who found
Nothing unusual

Except I suspect
That too
Has to do
With my unusual anatomy

Two eyes to see outward
Two to see inward
The vast of life
The spirit affords me
In dreams and visions
And mysteries
That outer sight cannot read

And eyes to hold
The ceaseless volumes
Of poems and prose
And peculiar mysteries
Recorded from the unknown

The manuscripts
And written word
From sermons
Songs
And years
Of journaling
Life

Two eyes to see in darkness
What rare eyes cannot
Decipher
In well-lit places

Ears to hear the natural
And two to hear the inaudible
My lot
My life
My gifts to others

Strange as it might sound
Is rooted in profundity
The enigma
That merits
No explanation
Beyond the curiosity
Of strangers

My tongue
The pen of a ready writer
A smaller piece attached
Seemingly
By an accidental incision
Left dangling
But examined more closely
Appears a miniature
Of the larger

What gifts God has bestowed
From rivers that swallow
To abundance
Of the tongue

Declaring
Life or death
Sickness or health

Wealth or poverty
Joy or sorrow
Praying
Prophesying
Reversing the edits
Of reciprocity

Singing
Shouting
Rebuking the error
Of profanity

Blessing
Or cursing
Exhorting truth
Or exfoliating lies
Persuading
Provoking
Living out loud

The tongue
The silver lining
Behind dark clouds

Apples of gold
In portrait of gloom
A comfort in distress
Distress in comfort
Declaring words of wisdom
To fools
Steadfast
Unmovable

The rudder that guides the ship
Across oceans
Celebrates
And honors
Defeats death with a word
Resurrects hope
With a song
Carries the banner of faith
Upon the wings of a poem
Extolling the virtues of God
Surrendered in worship
To unknown tongues
And languages that
Adore in reverence

Great the power of the tongue
I've been blessed to express
One the spiritual and the sacred
The other the oracles
Of the secular

The price I pay
I can't expound
To live inside the mind of God
To be stalked by devils
Impotent of power
To abort my purpose
I am not eulogized
I am crowned
There is no pity for the valleys
No penchant for the mountain
Or the arrest of fallow
Intentions
I have no desire for the honor of men
Lest I fall from this place
Enwalled in pride

Eye have not seen
Ear have not heard
Neither has it been revealed
To those who hate
Without a cause worthwhile

Extracting
Extravagance
From His bosom
Implanted in an earthen vessel
Named Doris
Remembering my youth
That Sabbath morn
When a child yielded
To the clarion call
Who shall I send
And who shall go for us

I stood
In awkward timidity
I could not then
Or now
Defend

Still I came to the altar
with strangers
Harboring the secrets of their fears
And the errors of their past
Who shall I send
And who shall go for us
Enters the faint voice of a child
Here am I, Lord
Send me
Unwavering
In my position

They wrapped a white sheet
Around my decision
And pronounced me
A candidate
For water baptism

Baptist water
Free will and freewheeling
Not to be confused
With Pentecostal fervor
Holy Rollers
They called them
For lack of discerning

Five years later
I would stand with them
Saved
Sanctified
Holy Ghost beaming

Life filled with contradictions
But not paradoxical
What seemed ambiguous
Was reconcilable
My heart was stern
And my face made flint

For all of what
Conversion consists
Healing
Body soul and spirit

The walls of my heart
Expanded
The place of my tent enlarged
He strengthened my stakes
And lengthened my cords
My capacity and patience
For people evolved
And life as I knew it
Surrendered to God

My lips
My tongue
My ears and teeth
My heart
And mind
My hands and feet
Multiplied…

January 11, 2011

Certain things we expect
In the realm of the atmosphere
Winter across the wintersphere
Did I just hear
That every state in the nation
Has snow simultaneously
Is that even possible?

Some places crushed by blizzards
And tempestuous storms
No wizardry
Or strand of wisdom
Can accurately predict
What only God controls
Like last year's pounding
Of the East coast
Nature compounded winter's fury
With unprecedented weather

From Texas to Maine
Even in places
Usually warm

Now two years counting
Georgia has snow
Can you believe it Lord
Of course you know

The tires of an 18-wheeler
In the clutch of nature's work
Their imposing statue
And highway bullying
Came to a gripping halt
Frozen on icy roads
Immobile
Along the freeway
Now shut down for safety

Thousands of power outages
Hundreds of flights grounded
Media warnings
To stay inside
Unless in case of extreme
Emergencies
Your fully loaded road ranger
Or winterizing
Is no match for Mother Nature
She holds creation in her grip
Steel and rubber
Is no exception

She topples trees
Upward from roots
And leaves them
Languishing in awkward spaces
Icy streets bear
Tire imprinted treads
Or the footprints of children
In frozen patches
Along walkways
Marking playful moments
Of joy that soon fades

January 12

The mind wills and devises evil
The same evil that turns adversary
And plunges the soul
Into the abyss of despair
What does it profit
To reach the pinnacle of desire
Only to still be insatiable
Still filled with the same
Anguish of emptiness
As when the soul
First conceived debauchery

What then
Shall it profit to gain
The whole of pleasure
And be left deplete of purpose

To have sown the seed of deception
And bore the harvest of wretchedness
Of one's own demise
To die prematurely
Only for a few years
Of reigning in the soul
And dying in the spirit?
For an epitaph that reads
Here lies one
Who lived and died
That'

Repentance
Father

May I record my thoughts
About love and lost

I was to be with him
But could not
For in another life
I had taken what could never be
I crossed the line of principle
Wrought with thoughts
Borrowed from the other me
I partook in what was not

Those chained and bound
Pursued me as though free
And I cautioned my soul
Then paused
And resumed the folly of the chase

Then paused again
To listen to my heartbeat
Against my fleeing
I penned a letter
That never left my hand
To remind me
He was not mine
I was not his

For a time it went
As I had planned
But never a dream
Could I have dreamed
That desire not destroyed
Will rise again

So it was
The longing amid pain
That left my heart
Like driftwood
Floating upon waters
Without compass of soul
Except lost...

There is none to blame
No finger to point
That does not return to me
I take full responsibility
It was I
Who at last
My own thoughts
I could not bear
The piteous footsteps
Upon my path
The reckless breathing of desire

The whimsical flirt with danger
The cause and effect
That renders the purest heart
Fallible

How and why
Does and can
The soul purges itself from sin?

January 11, 2011

I have enough love to sustain the wait
Enough patience
To accommodate your pace
Faith enough to continue with doubt
Facing what I see or not
Enough hope
To birth strands of light
Where dark patches
Lurk to haunt

I have enough assurance
To compensate wavering
Peace
Unshaken by intimidation
I have time enough
To stay the course
Strewn with promise
Enough truth to redeem
Today's tomorrow

I have the key that unlocks
The power of the heart
And binds
The will of soul
 Life and death
Are in the power of the tongue
But the heart of the king
Is in the hands of the Lord

January 13

Thank you Lord
For the purging of my lips
To speak prophetically
Into the atmosphere
To deliver what was
Heretofore hidden
Veiled
Unspoken
Forbidden to ears
Denied existence
In the natural realm

My lips
A vehicle of conveyance
Speaking forth
The mind of the Spirit
Bridging
Earth and heaven

Reverencing the sacred
Renouncing the rest
Leading the blind
Through parched and dry
Places
Devoid of voice
This is my repentance
For sins committed
Against the gateway
To the temple

Your confidence I hold
I confess my soul
I yield my spirit
No weapon formed against me
Shall prosper

January 14, 2011

This year I will dance without bounds
Without explanations
Or regrets unfound

For every rejection endured
There will be celebration
Crowned with festive rejoicing
Immeasurable

Psalms will be heaped
Upon the barren
Overtaken by dreams
Laden with fatness

Widowhood
Will be redeemed with song
Every moment of solace
And silence
Resolved
And I will walk unrestrained
By time

And there will be laughter
For every contemplation
Whether or not I was able
To weather my storm
Among the loss of family
And friends who started
But abandoned ship
Along the journey

I will dance
For years forbidden
Written off
And invisible
Name removed from the bulletin
And forgotten

Accomplishments
Never honored
Obfuscated
Left for dead
Until the day
Of reckoning
When I will dance
on the mount of God
Unplugged
Unopposed

Transfigured
And transformed

For all to see
What was heretofore hidden
A best kept secret
Now made visible

And there will be a performance
Of unprecedented acclaim
Never touted
On any world stage

No Hollywood genius
Could have created such a script
Or choreographed
What will happen next

Elations
Reparations
O' happy Day
No Nobel
Oscar
Or Pulitzer can compare
To the magnum opus
God's about to declare
A limited edition
Unlimited in scope
My time preserved
In a prophetic loam

And there will be dance
Across every time zone
Stranger to stranger and
Neighbors unknown

Hope dead and fragile
Shall hear the call
And earth children will share
My unfettered waltz
Angels will escort me
In the presence of my enemy
From the back of the line
To front row center

And the custodian of time
Holding access forbidden
Will hand me the scroll
To read what is written
In tongues unknown

We are the songs
That bear you witness
Forty-thousand recorded
Dreams and visions
Two thousand poems
Three hundred sermons
Books of life
Compiled from journals

We are the exceeding
Abundant above all
You ever imagined
Asked or thought
The fruit of seed sown in dark
Prayers offered for solitary hearts

We are the pressed down
Shaken together
Running over in your bosom
The return of your investment
A thousand times over

For children you raised
But did not birth
The mystery dancer
Who prayed it forward
Declaring life
In desolate soil
Even now
We hear your voice

We are your works
Kingdom wrought
To overflow
Ending drought
We serenade your generous spirit
Acts of kindness
For strangers abandoned

Captivating doubt and unbelief
You changed the nature
Of the atmosphere
Distributing
Unconditional love
To children cast off and
Disinherited

With the enemy watching
Uninvolved
You pulled the lesser
Into your arms
And offered their soul
Unto your God

We are the fruit
Eyes couldn't see
The lamentations
Deaf couldn't hear
The favor that hireling
Couldn't comprehend
Because it belonged
To you not them

We are the brackets
Around your name
That lengthened your cord
And established your stakes
The exponential increase
Of your tents
The golden staff
That brands your ship

Daughter
You've touched
The hem of my garment
For those less strong
Was just not strong enough
Fettered by tradition
Beset by sin
You birth new life
Where dreams lie dead

Immured with passion
Stalked by doubt
Judging yourself
For falling short

We are the reward
Of contrition
The heart broken
Unto repentance

Open your vats
Stretch forth your hands
Woman of God
Become yourself

Your latter rain
More abundant than the former
We are the royal garment
Of your harvest

Now servant child
After years of confessing
The time has come
To declare your blessing
Multiplied
Increased
Heap upon heap
No enemies
No opposition
Steady your feet
For resurrection dancing

One of heavens best kept secrets
About to be disclosed
And there shall be dance
Out of control

January 22

When I was incubated
In the womb of God
Jesus walked my life
Before I was born
All of my times were in his hands
All of my days at his command
Before I lived any moment in birth
He had already walked
My journey on earth

Wherever I am
He's been there before
He took my destiny
Upon the cross
He walked the end
Of my day and path
He carried my burdens
Upon himself

He confronted the issues
That he found
Would impede the journey
Of those heaven bound
He marked every plan
And conspiracy
Designed to sabotage
My destiny

There goes the love
I stopped to fondle
The one I thought
I would never get over
There's the gate of hell
It put me through
The breach of soul
The burden of proof
Yet here I stand
Two thousand-eleven
Garments untouched
In the fire
Headstone snatched
From its place
Dead woman dancing
On her grave

There goes the demonic attack
That failed
The weapon launched
But didn't prevail

For there is Jesus
Creating my way
The crooked transformed
Into paths made straight
Briars and thistles
He bore as a crown
Because he lived
No fear bounds me
In defeat

February 14

I am eternally smitten by God
There is no earth man who can compete
With the love I have for him
Or he for me
If there is one who thinks he can
He walks a lie
Hopelessly
Self-deluded
Believing his own hype
Thinking himself to be
 Something he's not

For what man born of woman
Cast from genes of mere mortal
Can stand in the same sphere
As God
And not be dwarfed
To infinitesimal

He anticipates my needs
And creates the circumstances
To fulfill them

He knows my thoughts
Before I think them
He hears me before I call
And while I am still speaking
He has answered

My father
And God
Eternal friend
Faithful to a fault
They seek
But cannot find his error
They fail
Yet cannot endure his strength

He doesn't love
And leave me
His promises doesn't falter
His character doesn't alter

There is not one strand of abuse
Not one crack in his armor

He doesn't collect offenses
And use them against me
When I am weak
His strength undergirds me
Where he hides me
I cannot be found

When he reveals me
All will know
I am his bride
The apple of his eye
The sweet smell of perfection
In his nostrils

He chose the bride he would pursue
Then pursued me to surrender
With loving kindness
He entreated me
He broke the chains
That held love captive
And lifted me to my pinnacle

When I triumph
He is honored
Nothing makes him any prouder

His glory adorns me
In abject laughter
The least offense
Brings his thunder
When I'm wronged
He handles it

He sanctifies my tears with joy
Multiplies the seeds I sow
He adds peace
Subtracts sorrow
Guards the gate
Of my tomorrow

He brings no game
Just love unsurpassed
By any love-struck man
There is no competition
No need for taking numbers
Unless you dare to be mentored

By God
Here is where you can start
Love me
As he loved the Church
And gave himself for it
Pamper me
Like you do your own body
Lather me with oils
And lavender
Consume me breathless
Entreat me with kindness
Forgive me of my sins
Even when I'm guilty
Then take me into your arms
And hold me
Until I'm sorrowfully
Transformed

He adorns me in splendor
More radiant than nature
The finest silks and linen
Hand tailored

I ask
He upbraids not
Lavishing me endless
From the treasures of his heart
And his infinite genius
I've never a lack
He doesn't fulfill
And if ever he holds back
It's simply because
What I've desired is beneath
What He desires for me

From the vastness of his gifts
I claim my portion
Transported from His eternal
Generosity of spirit
He illuminates me
With his own brilliance
And gives me what
No man can tender

This is my challenge
To the earthborn husband
Who wonders
Why I worship you flawless

Answer me when I call
Indulge my desires
Speak of me proudly
Trust the love I offer
Without conditions
Shower me with gifts
I never expected

Love the man child I bore
Who doesn't bear your name
Father him
Enlarge him
Cover my shame

Be the pride of my daughter
Put the twinkle in her eye
Not the rod of a tyrant
That draws blood for mistakes

Honor me
For bearing you children
For multiplying your name
Heaping dignity upon your legacy

Romance me when I age
When the perfection of youth
Fades into laugh lines
And looseness
Be the love of my life
As promised

Do not break your vows
Be true to your covenant
Your children watch
For the best example

Marry me
Point me out in the marketplace
Make me the envy of every woman
Who seeks to be adorned with praise
Let the brethren envy you
For the way we are

Cover me
Bone of your bone
Flesh of your flesh
So I'm hidden from every enemy

Lead me into the destiny
That's ours to conquer
That we might leave the imprint
Of purpose

Do not I pray
Lead me without a dream
Without the sheer profoundness
Of discovery

The world is too vast
Help me to seize it
To claim my place
Among its inhabitants

I will follow you to greatness
But I will not follow mediocrity
I will dance to your song
But I will not bow to frivolity

I will cast caution to the win
Only as a treat
For enjoying the journey
Do not bore me with apathy
Cry if you must
But do not pout
It's unflattering
For any man of statue
Err on the side of faith
And not procrastination
Lead me and I will follow
To a certain destination
Or uncertain
As long as there is purpose

Show me the world God made
Introduce me to other nations
Races and
Cultures

God does that
As certain as he is God
If you come close to my expectations
I will oblige your generosity
Your penchant for beauty

Searching hidden
And unknown wonders
And amazements of nature
He rewards my faith
With gratuities
Beyond my grandest imagination
His promises are as certain
As the sunrise

He doesn't err in the dark
Doesn't make mindless blunders
There is simply no rivals
No competition to cite
Not one or a host
Gone or coming

He doesn't forget anniversaries
Or the day I was born
Doesn't whimper and whim
Like some spoiled little boy
Honey, I forgot
Too busy
Too insensitive
Too Stingy

Not enough anticipating
Far too less attention
Too caught up in the Super Bowl
To know I existed
Just chillin with the fellows
Have a cold 40

Smacking his lips
On Nachos and hot wings
While God watches over me
And the children

He sends his word
And I'm strengthened

He searches for the pain of heart
He knows when I am hurting
In him I live and have my being
In me he stores his treasure
The opulence of gifts
Enviable

Regal to the eye
Palpable to the touch

When I enter
I hear their whispers
Who is she
She belongs to Him
Him...
No not him
Him...
Him who?

The Him you can't approach
Can't hold a candle to his I Am ness
Dwarfed by his bigness
The Him you deny
The Him you reject
Or relegate to "give me"

Blaspheme
Or neglect in prayer
The Him you study
But will never know
Because you're too busy
Worshipping yourself
Seeking Him
Is benign consideration
Always searching
Never obtaining

The Him you label nonexistent
Resisting his advances
To pull you into his bosom
Like her
The Him you use
And discard
Without regard to sacred wooing
Abandon on the altar
Because you tire
Of calling in vain
And He doesn't answer

Him who you left
To pursue a lover
A lover
Who now you cannot find
And so you move on to another
Abuse again
And then
You cry to Him
Him who?
Not him
Him…

The Him whose garment
You cannot touch
Whose shoes
You cannot untie
Him
Whom you betray
With earthen gods

Supping in splendor
With idols
Who turn and rend you
Leave your children naked
For debts you cannot oblige

Him
Who satisfies my mouth
With delicacies
Renews my youth
Like the eagles
Defends me against every enemy

Whose love
Leaves me speechless
Not grievous and
Uncovered like a whore

Misunderstood
And uncared for
Swept away by lies
And conditions on demand
No tolerance for mistakes
Control without benefits
Altering my DNA
Without altering his
Changing the way I look
Hating who I am

Submitting
Still
Left for dung
For someone else
Not half as good

Give me Him
Who in sovereignty adorned
Immortal
Invisible

Granting dignity for scorn
Raising from the ash pile
Where men have left trampled
Transforming
Clothing beauty for ashes

Weeping may endure for a night
But He brings me
Morning joy

The earthborn comes
And stakes his claim
In hearts he cannot heal
Refusing to love beyond
His own desires
Cannot make whole

He takes what he cannot restore
Plunders the soul of its good
And cannot replenish
Not all
But most

This marring of character
Refusing to worship
But desiring to be

"I am your god,
Obey me?

But at the end
He stumbles
And falters
Simply because
He cannot compete

His offer at best
Will only last for a day

An invitation
To a Buck's game
An IM of a single
Red rose
Two brief conversations
To say "thank-you"
I love you
Withheld

Hovering
Apprehensively
In the atmosphere
Clinging to the fear
Of rejection
And deformed manhood

Hurt
Wounds still opened
Scar tissue
Exposed to scrutiny
Love just a fable
For fools
A chance encounter
Between strangers

Or past hearts
Now estranged
Separated by offenses
Not easily forgotten

Valentines
Turned vexation
Love abandoned
Without possibility
Of renewal
No second chances
No rewrites
Romance
Withered

Excuses abused
Time out used

Forgiveness
Mistaken for stupidity
Silence
But not serenity
Surrender
But not victory
Compromise
But not cowardice
Lonely
But not alone
Heart aching
But not broken

Disappointed
But not devastated
Shaken
But not shattered
Life force
Threatened
But still intact

Confidence tested
But not eroded
Hope still clings to faith
Faith still
Working by love

Love remains
The greatest of all
Human
And
Divine encounters

It has taken some learning
Some purging
Of fallacies
Intense difficulties
And extraordinary
Challenges
To birth this certainty

I have but one
True valentine
One eternal flame
That will never
Be extinguished
By pain
Or comfort
Happiness
Or sorrow

Failure
Or success
Weariness
Of spirit
Rest
Or toil

Triumph
Or tragedy
Fame
Or infamy
Wealth
Or poverty

His love
Unconditional
His character
Unimpeachable
His promise
Unbreakable

His cell
Never busy
He's always reachable

So as long as
I do not break
The communion
His grace abounds

His loyalty
Unquestionable
His word is a tower
His tongue
A quenching fire
The Father of truth
He cannot lie

When He says
"I love you"
It's infallible
Immutable
An indisputable reality

No hidden agenda
Or ulterior motives
He's not being deceitful
Or trying to control you

It's real
Take it to the bank
No greater love
Than His to confess

Gentle
Kind
Alms giving
Compassionate
Leading
In constructive wisdom
Anchored
In faith

Driven by purpose
Not swayed by conventions
Or deterred by trouble

His arm not short
His ears not heavy
Protector of children
Honoring women

Hated for his perfection
In Him I ascend
To the greatness
I was born
Beyond mediocre
To my statue as a woman

I am His
He is mine
Life is full
With my true valentine

February 26, 2011

Father
I saw one of yours today
It happened right here
Where we raise our proud voices
Amid ledgers and scrolls
That herald the lives
Of the triumphant

A woman
Wheelchair bound
Trying not to evoke pity
Passes silently amongst
The cacophony of history
Unnoticed
As I suppose she intended
Or perhaps not

The clanging
of the wheelchair pedals
Spoke volumes to the listless silence
And shifting eyes
Avoiding her calamity
The toil of struggling

"I am over here."
Yelled the wheelchair's clatter
My rider's legs are frail
How will she ever make it
Wheeling me backwards
One awkward micro movement
At a time
It will take forever."

She is not dead
As reports had it
It was just a rumor
Circulating

Premature prayers
That fell on deaf ears
Turned silent
Her times have been extended
You cannot think her dead
With disdainful eyes
Or enchantments
That leave the mouth dry
She lives
To awaken the heart to compassion

To arouse from sleep
And apathy
To set the soul on fire
With caring

She sits badly slumped
In the rickety wheelchair
Paddling her feet
Against the gravity
Of the coarse carpet
And the frailness of health
From what appeared a recent stroke
Right side weakened
Her hand went limp at the risk

Still she braved her way
Along the book table path
A host of ardent readers
Scholars
Geeks on assignment
From boredom
Loiterers with nowhere
Specific to go

Even the librarian
Cast a certain eye

Did anyone notice her clumsy presence
Fill their peripheral vision
With two soiled wash cloths
Wrapped around the handles
Of the wheelchair
A white gauze around her
Dangling ankle

How did she get here
And how would she leave
I wondered
Watching with curiosity
Men passing their mother
Students their teacher
Women
Turning their eyes away
From a suffering sister

One fellow human being
After another
Was just too busy
Or preoccupied to care

Busy..,
Researching social change
Busy...
Reading biographies
Of world changers
Busy...
With thesis
And dissertations
To qualify
For a PhD
Doctorates
of divinity
Letters of high acclaim
Busy...
Ignoring the call of greatness
Veiled in disability

"Ma'am,"
I approached with quiet indignation
Do you need help getting somewhere
Here let me turn your around
Let me push you
Where you need to go

She pointed to the checkout
I released the footrest
And gently guided her feet onto it
"Now" I said
"Isn't that a lot better?"
She raised her head
To meet my eyes
Her smiled widened
She said
"A lot better"

We stopped at the counter
And I lifted the oversized GED reference
From her lap
And handed it to the librarian
I watched as she secured
Her card in her bag
As I turned her to exit

"How did you get here?"
"The transportation" she responded
In slurred forced speech
"They will be returning to get me,
Shortly."

"Where will they meet you?"
"Downstairs."
She tried to point

But her finger barely moved

I pushed her slowly into the hallway
To the elevator
To piercing stares
And sympathetic glaring
I guided the chair
Up the steep corridor
To the side entrance
The cold biting Wisconsin winter
Rushed in behind
The opening and closing of the door

I pulled her coat
Tight around her trembling shoulders
And guided her arms into the sleeves
She settled into the warmth
Of a stranger's kindness
I could not leave her alone

Waiting
So I stood by as she made her call
 Until my concerns for her safety
Were answered
By the arrival of the transit
One hour later...

June 8, 2011

Last night I dreamed
Beautiful thoughts
They floated across my screen
Like butterflies
On crested wings
They lured me into their charm
And held me captive
With mysteries
Unfolding
Seamlessly
I grabbed the challis
Of their wings
And held tightly the arm
Of the dancing ballerina

Scenes opened and closed
And I followed their bidding
Down the endless skyline
Of chase and illusion
Until they eluded
My shifting eyes
And the noises of the night
Consumed their being

The blowing of the fan
The humming of a light
A cough
Or a sneeze

Or the call of the alarm
And the restless protest
Of body toil

Footsteps on squeaky stairs
Or broken tile
The slight close of a door
The gentlest turn of a key
Trying unsuccessfully
Not to arouse from sleep

Even the crickets added their voice
To the conspiracy to disconnect
Dreamers from their visions
Serenading the morning
In a Capella arrogance
Until all that is left
Are fragmented images
Which I hold steady
But could no more remember
Until the most vivid detail
Is snatched away
By the sound and fury of the night

And I awake
From all but peaceful sleep
And ask. Why?

July 3. 2011—Our Song

Lord...
I want to deliberately
Spend time with you
With purpose of heart
Spirit to spirit
To feel the touch
Of your presence
To hear the thunder of your voice
Against the beat of my heart
To see the fire in your soul
And the depth in your eyes
I want to deliberately
Worship you

Deliberately
Spend time with you
Not just a passing hello
I will see you after while
But O, my Father
By design

I want to make a date with you
A time and place for us to talk
I will wait if you are late
Or you get there before I do
Charge it to my head
And not my heart

Doris Wellington

I want to sit at your feet again
Feel your hand gently caress my head
As my soul cry out for you
The way it used to do…

I want to hear you enter the room
Where I've been waiting for you
See the brilliance
That transcends all
That life offers or gives
I want to deliberately
Spend time with you

I don't need a fancy meeting place
Don't need to light candles
Or sprinkle incense
Around the room

I Don't need fancy clothes
Or new suede shoes
Just want to spend time
With you

You are the song
Of my heart
In you I live
Move
And have my being
Without your presence
I can't walk among them

So hold out your hand
Let me fill them again
Open your heart
I will pour mine into yours
Come to me
Rain or shine
Snow or hail
Sun or moon
Here or there
Come to me

I want to see your smiling eyes
Look into mine
I want you to give me
Your signature high five
When I've done something
That pleases you to laughter
Even the angels talk about
The time we spend together
As they move the universe
To do my spoken will
You only need to come
And I will meet you there

You choose the place
I'll choose the time
You choose the time
I'll choose the place

Doris Wellington

Your thoughts are mine
My thoughts are yours
We are a team

Together
Unbeatable

My friend
My child
My daughter
Princess among Kings
Priest among power
Royal to the eyes
Even they can't see
What you mean to me
.
Thank You Father
I feel so undeserving of that kindness
That you just spoke to me
I feel I've let you down
And shouldn't be given such favor
Such consideration
So much gentleness
That's what I miss
That's why I choose
To deliberately
Spend time with you.

August 15, 2011
(Confronting the Spirit of Jezebel)

Lord,
What must I do?
Her anger spews salty venom
Keys protest against broken tile
I bow
Picked them up
With no verbal display
Of such vile disregard
Of sanctity

Rearing its head
To exert position
But I do not buy into her desire
To live two lives—
Hers and mine
Without sacrificing control of one
To live the other

If but one were God's
I would be thoroughly satisfied
That though we exist
Between two worlds
We can but live one life
God's—
Not me hers
Not her mine

So, she seeks to consume mine
With tempestuous envy
Because of the life
I surrendered
For the one I now live
If but for a moment to own
Clinging to the core
Of its purest suffering
That thrusts me upon the altar
Of self-denial to own it
To claim it
In the darkest chambers
Of isolation
Me and it
Codependent

That I might live
Beyond the miring madness
Of mere Christianity
And live this life
She seeks to inhabit

The endless meddling
Into a world she will never control
Because there is no earth puppet
Attached to the strings she dangles
That which she seeks
Has long abandoned
The mundane desire
Of pleasing flesh
And responds
Only to that voice
That gently leads this servant
Through the valley
Of the shadow of death

To the only life I've know
Since the call
Of the Spirit's bidding
Where he leads
I'm compelled to follow

So she compounds her disgust
Into blatant acts of denial
Refusing to do
What is inherently right
No call to breakfast
Car fuel left on empty
No questions as to the needs
Once eager to meet
Or requesting the fellowship
Of laughter

Things shared among friends
When Jezebel is not present
Now strained
To send the message
 I hold the keys to your provision
In a land where you live among strangers

Notwithstanding her faulty emoting
She is the victim
I—the villain
In this charade
Created by the delusion
That we are equals

I am the teacher
She is the pupil
She can no more live my life
Than I can live hers
Or even bring her to understand
That death held with contempt
For the ordinary and yearns
Piteously to know
But one
Waiting the approaching dusk
Where dreams give way to dreams
Too numerous to catch
Too God to understand
Too simple to ignore the life of leading

When one feels no need or desire
To impart life
From the very fountain
She refuses to ingest

All other contenders
For my obedience
Do not exist

I hear the rattle of their voices
I see the wagging of their tongues
But they are invisible to me
I cannot follow what cannot be seen
They were not there
Among the graven ashes
And tears
Of solitary confinement
Sucked dry of self-indulgence

Everything she possesses
And holds dear
In protective jealousy
I have surrendered

A job that assures that she will eat
When at dusk
Night wraps its arms around her night
She will sleep
Recline to the comforts of life
That job provides for husband
And dependent children

And I will fall asleep
In the arms of a faith

And yield my spirit
An empty cistern
My soul a blank canvas
Upon which the Spirit will write
And pour his mind into my surrender

But no calls will come
From my earth children
For they do not exist
I gave them to You
While they were in the womb
So that I could give birth
Beyond the death
Of mortal souls
And these do call
From time to time
But I do not wait for them
For they too
Are not mine

Tears will fall evenly upon my pillow
While she and her house watch
Madea's Family Reunion
For the thousandth time

Technology brings the ease of touch
Blue ray, DVD players
And High-Def computers
Blackberries
I Phones
Platinum TV"s
Flat screens in almost every room inhabited
Thousands of movies

The latest release never denied
For it's coming soon
One way or another
Blockbusters, Walmart
Netflix or Red Box

The rock guards the yard
And the garage that stores
The excess of things acquired
Outdated toys
Bicycles
Mopeds
And Harleys
That glow in the dark
An extra auto just for travel
A pick-up and two commercial vehicles

Still she craves
The carefree life of not knowing
Answering to no husband
But God

And there are the children
Grandchildren
Given lawful through marriage
Or sacrificed to serve God
Who are my mother's children?
The ones I left behind
To answer the call
From one tryst or another
To places unknown

There are no children
Except the ones
I collected in the service
Of the Lord

I do not complain of being without
As when I was young and barren
For now I've come to know
You gave me children I have not born

There has been no sacrifice
That does not return
Multiplied
Children I did not birth
Rise up and call me mom
A people I did not know
Stand up to serve me
When one defaults
Another will rise
And go the distance

Still, some begrudge
What I have
Who I am
Compared to what?

To whom is it given
To measure the distance
Of sacrifice and surrender
Who can weigh the depth of loneliness
Bequeath the soul

Or the volume of a heart
Rendered full
Yet empty of what others treasure?

I am more bound than they are free
Freer than they are bound
Yet she envies my carefree chains
Not knowing where I will rest
Or open my soul to strangers

No permanent address
So many dwellings
It is daunting
Yet my age
Is not easily determined
By the temple that
Houses this nomad
Who follows the call of God
To the cry of the people
Believing for compassion

Planting a seed of gratitude
Which is never just recompense
For services rendered

Only God can do the arithmetic
He calibrates the misgivings
The denial of good
When the bowels of compassion
Are shut against me

Who can quantify the value
Of true labor
The impartation of gifts
Beyond human measure?

How can one fix the price
For turning the wayward feet forward?
Or laying hands on the sick unto recovery
Hurling a new word
To reshape the future
Of the desolate
And casting off the yoke of demons
Stalking to possess the soul
And dispossess the spirit
Counseling to prosperity
And turning dishonor to destiny

Who but God understands
The cost of the preached word
Standing upon concrete barriers
Sunday after Sunday
Calling those things that are not
As though they were
Dissecting
Unveiling

Illuminating
God to children

What is the worth
Of prayers whispered
In the vortex of silence
To cover the despairing lives of family
Out of order
Children scaling the walls backwards
While I reverse the curse

And foil the enemy's plans
Standing in the gap
Between good and evil
Baptizing the repentant soul
Or those
Who thought themselves so
Serving the Eucharist
In desolate places
Proclaiming life
Where death had wreaked havoc

And those simple services
That are overlooked
By human error

And the selfish indulgence
Of the eye

Looking
But not seeing
Listening
But not hearing
Present in body
Absent in mind
Perception obscured
By a hidden agenda
Ears clogged by the noise of the benign
Presence removed
By the unintentional
Disregard or ignorance
In the pride of life
Do they not know
Have they not heard
I have stood upon the fat
Of the feet of angels
Who carried my youth
Across the chasm of dusk
Into a new morning

gave me to You
A mere child
You gave me back
Multiplied
Portions plump
And full of life

I gave you thirteen
Childhood poems
You gave me back
Thirteen thousand more
I gave you inchoate ability
You gave it back
In dreams and visions
Too vast to number
To God to dismiss

I laid my plans upon the altar
You gave them back
Laden with purpose
The gift of praise
And profound wisdom
The answer to petitions
I'm yet to utter

I sacrificed the pursuit of the letter
You filled my soul
With enviable treasures
Hidden from the wise and prudent
For which they search
In futility

I stripped my earthly garment bare
You covered me with righteousness
I offered the simple prayer of faith
You gave me the world to change
Earth daughter
Of Africa born
Feet shod with holy oil
Lips anointed with hieroglyphics
Poured from my Father's Spirit
My tongue the pen
Of a ready writer
Unfolding mysteries
Spoken in secret

O spirit of Jezebel
Taking what is not yours
Soul slain by the sword of God

Birthing children who have
No form
Futures shaped
By misconception

Destinies
Aborted in the belly
Jealous to a dying fault
Now scorn the thing
Seduction has wrought

The love of money
The blood of harlotry
Cast yourself
Upon your altar
The one you erected
To worship yourself
Open wide your grave
Receive yourself

I am blood born
Adopted
I carry the seal
Of my righteous Father
My DNA incorruptible

Baptized
Into a divine covenant
I act out the power
I have inherited

If this is what
They envy of me
I offer myself again to thee
Fill my cup to overflow
Give them more to be jealous for

September 26, 2011

1996
You birthed a word
In my spirit
I Waltzed with God
The Morning of Genesis
Fifteen years later
You give it back
A cast of one hundred fifty
The whistles and bells
Of an epic
Colorful and splendid awe

Still I captured
What I saw
In your presence

 I marvel
At a time that pushes
Me onto the stage of promise

The birthday gift
Of a dream come true
Is why I've sowed my life in You
You lay me down and get me up
In thee O'Lord
I put my trust

I will not die before I wake
For in thee O'God
My future is safe
I anchor my faith in Thee alone
There is no exit
Until I am done

The latter rain
Overpowering the former
The answer
Overtaking the promise
The harvest knocks
On the door of the seed
And gushes forth
While time concedes

My name is etched in your hands
Nothing can impeach my time
I hear the thrust of the wind
From every direction
Reminding me
That the best is coming
No delay
No waiting in line
Plain and simple
It's my time

I here release
The yoke of past
The weight of those
Who held me fast

The words I spoke
They did not honor
Yet they expect
To reap my harvest
I shake the dust from my feet
And seize the day you kept for me

I hear the rushing
Mighty wind
It is time
To let it in

October 6, 2011

Father
Forgive me of my sin
I have fallen short
Of your glory again
Here I am
Not to complain
But to seek understanding
Perhaps to vent

How can children
From the same womb
The same bloodline
The same empty spoon

Children of scorn
Who knew no honor
Except it came
From the one mother
The center of hope
The anchor in storm
When each other's joy
Was all we owned

How can those
Who walked and talked
The same path
Poverty strewn
From house to house

Eating from one hand
Then turn and rend
The ox that once
Gave them bread

How can they refuse to honor
The very thing that gave them
Earth breath
Affirming their life
Shielding from death
How can they forget?

October 15, 2011

How can they forget?
The God
In my mother's house
The picture she framed
Still hangs in my heart
The voice of God
Still resounds
Through the corridors
Once filled with shame
Now redeemed

The soft pillar
Still rest upon the floor
Beneath the window
Where we once bowed
To beseech the Lord
Our mother's God

Our Father
Which art in heaven
He shall reign forever and ever
And Lead us not into temptation
But deliver us from all evil
Lord, make us one

Make us to lie down
Besides green pasture
I still hear
Your sacred laughter
Piercing our sorrow

The family Bible
Still beckons me pause
Its tattered cord
Hails its power
In the beginning was the word
And the word was with God
And the word was God
The same was in the beginning with God

And God said,
Let there be...
And there was
And the Word became flesh
And dwelt among us
And we beheld his glory
Unblemished

By faith we understood
That the worlds were framed
By the word of God
And that our own faith
Was shaped by the words
Written of the God
She worshipped and served

Have they forgotten
Her dinner prayers
Lord we thank you for this food
We are about to receive
For the nourishment of our bodies
For Christ's sake
Amen

Or...

The prayers around the bed
Now, I lay me down to sleep
I pray the Lord my soul to keep
If I should die before I wake
I pray the Lord
My soul to take
Amen
Goodnight
Thank the Lord

Were they not there with me
Did they not hear
Our mother teach
Honor thy father and mother

This is the first commandment
That promises
To extend our days

Did they not hear a mother's plea
He who walks with the wise
Shall be wise
But a companion of fools
Shall be destroyed
Train up a child
In the way he should go
And when he is old
He will not depart

Did they not hear her cries for us
A thousand midnights of tears
When there was no bread
No work
No husband to comfort her
Travail
I can still hear the intercession
In my mother's house

A stream of light
Flows through
The closed door
Of the cramped bathroom
Where her invocations
Shifts to groans
All my children
Shall be taught of the Lord
And great shall be the peace
Of my children
They shall return
From the enemy's camps
Back to their own borders

The walls still bulge with praise
The plaster of Paris
Still stand amazed
Of her song

Holy Ghost
Don't leave me
Holy Ghost
Please, don't leave me
Holy Ghost
Don't leave me
Guide me along my way

The choir loft swayed and rocked
As she paced across
The small space
Behind the preacher's head

Somebody all time
Talk'n about me
But really
I don't mind
The mean things they say
Don't make me feel bad
Can't miss a friend
That I never had
He's pleading for me

A poor humble sinner
On earth here I am
My only hope lies
In the blood of the lamb
Wonderful
Counselor
Now stands in court above
With the power to save
And a heart full of love
He's pleading for me...

Did they forget Christmas Eve?
Fighting winter at twenty degrees
So we could celebrate
The birth of Jesus
And have a meal to eat

Hail to the South
Cotton has come
Let us receive the king
Crowned with indignities
Embellished with deception
Masked
As the American Dream

Our feet are numb
Our bellies empty
Our bodies jaded and bent
But there will be no food
Beyond these fields
Unless this cotton we pick

Mudd and dad
Taking the front
Children
Bringing up the rear

Together we need seven hundred pounds
To pay the lights and rent

Whatever is left
Mudd will decide
What meal we'll have tomorrow
Baked chicken
And cornbread
Or
Gourmet dressing
And turkey

A chocolate cake
Made from scratch
Or real banana pudding
Potato salad
And the choice between
Cabbage
Or collard greens

She will work through the night
Scribbling names on paper bags
And throwing wood
Into the fire
To keep her promise warm

Cut out puzzles
For the boys
Lincoln logs
Perhaps
Jump ropes
For the girls
Paper dolls or Jacks

An orange
An apple
A candy cane
Pecans
And peanut brittle

A proud mother
Assesses her work
Making sure
No name is missing

Then quietly at the break of dawn
She lays her body down
With the prayers she whispered
Through the night
Finally, the work is done

O' cramped
Fragile
Shotgun house
How still we see her lie
Above a mother's restless sleep
She still remembers God

Today
I wake to a rainbow
Flowing through a prism
Of broken colors
Scattered around the room
Courtesy of the morning sun
I follow the light
To a place
Where I could quietly embrace
The promises
My Father made
And kept
In my mother's house

She ate the scraps
We ate the bread
Portions rationed out to twelve

She patted her flat tummy
"I'm trying to watch my weight"
But the truth she would not tell
She sacrificed her right to eat
Until her children were fed

I know it was a choice of will
But whose will
Hers or God's
We might never understand
Why she held our lives
Higher than hers
When mockers scoffed
She raised her voice
"I'm having these children
For God."

They'll stand and teach
And prophesy
And preach the word of God
They'll sing and shout
From the mountaintop
They'll dance
On fallow ground

Earth will yield the harvest of
The word which she declared
Pastors
Prophets
Weavers of dreams
Her legacy holding fast

Love one another
Follow your convictions
For all the world to see
That among all earthborn
Who boasts of greatness
There is none greater than she

A highway shall be there
And a road
The way of Holiness
The path shall unfold before you
Strewn with my mother's prayers

This morning I rose
To my mother's voice
There is still God
In my mother's house

In me
He lives
In me He moves
In me he has His being
I am the harvest of my mother's faith
The answer to my mother's prayers

3:34P
Can anyone dream higher than the mother
No...No...and No again

October 22, 2011

Is there anything more magnificent than God?
The heavens that leave speechless
Those replete with adjectives
For every phenomenon
Holds captive billions
Of galaxies
That are as different as
The fold of clouds that veil them
Secret from the eye
                        Is but an imprint
Of the magnificence of God

There is nothing to compare
For all things bear his signature
Nothing in competition
Nothing to envy
It is all his
It all comes from him
Shaped by infinite wisdom
That created every color
In the spectrum of prisms
Through which lights and
Colors all the world
We experience

Unspeakable beauty
Birthed from the brute force
Of lava
Rushing to the surface
Of the Krakatoa
Erupting
Transforming the landscape
Into billowing smoke
Dreadful
Gripping the eye
Smoldering beauty

Deadly to the ear
Traveling
Across twelve percent
Of the world sphere
Still...
The mystique

Not even
Niagara Falls
With all its allure
And a resplendent rainbow
Draped across a chasm
Of boisterous waves
That flows endlessly
Between two countries
Can compare

11-12-10

Do not airbrush me with deceptions
Or lift my face to hide the toil
Do not reconfigure my cheek
Or tighten the skin around my bones
Leave the rugged strain of night
The uneven tones of sacrifice
Remove not the glaze from my eyes
Or trace the lines around my smile

These are the trophies
Of my spirit
The testimony
Of grace and resilience
I've walked against the roar of wind
Turned rivers red with my tears
My lips are cracked
No moisture bleeds through
Lipstick camera poised
So do not try to resurrect
What has died
A thousand times purged with fire

Let my countenance of years gone by
Showcase my passage
From death to life
Leave bare my scars for all to see
No closed casket for me…

November 14, 2011
My Tarrying Song

Thirty-eight years ago
I bowed my knees on a concrete floor
At the church by the railroad tracks
A lopsided picture of Jesus
Hung behind the podium
A vague shadowy figure
Of a woman approached
And Kneeled beside me
I heard David Penn's fleecing God
Concerning his call to ministry
"If Sister Rachael raises her hand
Three times
I'm a minister!"

Yes....I want to pray with him
Lift my voice above the worn snare
My brother is banging
While singing off key

"If I can help somebody as I travel along
Then my living will not be in vain."

The supplicants joined him in the chorus
"Then my living will not be in vain"
And I raised my ignorant innocence
Up to God and cried
Until salt tears watered my longing

Save me O'Lord!
I am a sinner
Of no fault of my own
Blame Adam
But don't leave me alone
On this altar of repentance
With no hope of being changed

Save, me O'Lord
From an alcoholic father
Dragging his demons
From generations gone by
To the center
Of our poverty-stricken existence

Save me
From the toil of cotton
And the smell of tobacco
Still branded in my flesh
Six years and counting

Save Me
From trying to help Mudd
Every time dad gets the urge
To pull that gun from his pocket
And threaten her
For no reason at all
Except he's a coward

Save me from the memory
Of jumping between
His loaded gun
And Mudd's raised hatchet
Fed up to the brim and overflowing
From taking his crap
Save Me
I'm lost without a future
So I skipped college
To hang around the house

I didn't trust that dad
Wouldn't do her harm
So I took a job
At Cameron Station for a while

And sure enough
In the midst of my mourning
I looked up just in time
Sister Rachael raised her hands
Three times
And then slowly
As Sister Willett opened the door
Pastor Wright rolled her eyes
I counted Sister Rachael's fourth
O' Lord save me from doubting
What do you want me to do now?

My throat is hoarse
From calling your name
My knees are knotted
From dank November floor
My fingers are numb from clapping
My teeth rattle from speed calling "Jesusssss!"
Without benefit of breathing
The louder the more believable

Save me from tarrying
From drowning in weary
Entertaining suicidal pity

For not knowing my purpose
And for still questioning
The color of God
Save me O'Lord
Before Christmas Eve
So that I will not be
An unbelieving heathen
With nothing to celebrate

It is my cry
My endless yearning
If there is God
Come and prove it
Right here
Right now
In the midst of my longing
In spite of my doubts
And reservations

Save me O' Lord
Lift up my head
Do not leave me I pray
To return to dad
Without salvation

And so I remember
As clearly as any visitation since

The rush of calm that entered my spirit
The cool ginger breathing against my cheek
Like the whispering pines of a quiet night

The strength of a force
I could not see
Lifted me upward upon my feet
As new tears
Cascaded upon the floor

The world stopped around me
And I raised my faith
As an offering unto the grace of God
"Those who call upon the Name of the Lord
Shall be saved"

And in that moment of my serene
That church by the tracks couldn't contain
What I'd just received
In immeasurable joy

Saved
To the upmost
I believed
From the sins of Adam
And the curse of Eve
(Whatever that means)
I am saved...

Saved
From needing to understand
About that and this
Or this and that
Too far in
I can't look back

And so I turned
To the vague
Shadowy figure of the woman
Eyes filled with tears
I hugged my mother's joy

Together we danced
Arm and arm
For she too
Had received the Lord

Thirty-eight years and county
We still eat
From his bounty
Mom and I
Still reverently speak
Of that night we received
Jesus Christ

11-22 7:30A

The human heart is designed for touch
A gentle stroke
That snatches from the brink
Of insanity
Those who sit in idle places
Nurturing self-hatred and loathing
For those loved

The human mind
Is meant to be interactive
Not hidden behind forbidden fantasies
Without engaging
With the world beyond its own

Trapped
Conceiving debauchery
Devouring madness
To be regurgitated
Upon festive dreamers
Pursuing life
Outside a realm
Where dreams die

And its inhabitants
Have long surrendered
To melancholy

The human spirit
 Is built for resilience
There is no room
No time for quitting
The spirit rises and soars
Falls and rises
Then stands
For a moment of contemplation
Devising new strategies

Turning failures
Into steppingstones
Taking bitter
And making better
Emerging from the shadow of victims
Clenching victory
With song

Dreams held secure
Even through the valley
Of the shadow of death

Defying fear
With continuance

The human will
Was designed for triumph
Divine DNA
Runs through our veins
There is no hardness
That we cannot with faith
Tame

We were built for endurance
This is our insurance
That God's investment
Is not wasted
By grumbling and complaining
About such as we have
The power to change

All else we conquer
By knowing the limit
Between God and man
So the wise
Seek his presence
Yearns the missing link
That's only found in relationship

A strange
Complex
Yet single surrender
As deliberate
As it is spontaneous

Still there remains a portion
We cannot claim
Except in God

The human being
Was meant to feel
To touch
To taste
To see and hear
Still we do not know
The intuitive nature
Of his being

No matter
The brilliance of man
There is a portion
Of the mantle
That can never be ours
Even if we should gain the world
The full measure of the soul
We will never understand

Doris Wellington

So while we sit in awe of ourselves
Measuring ourselves
By the statue of man

Who rises and falls
To the human will
Man is designed
To rise to heights
To fearlessly rule
In the strength of the lion

He waltzes gingerly with the lamb
Calms the savage paw of bears
He tames the jungle
And makes wild the tame

He navigates above the clouds
And charts the course of land

Every science
That can be pursued
He does so
Persistent
Enthused
Lingering long after the sun

Arising before the day begins
Flying with eagles
Running with gazelles
Swimming with sharks
Scaling walls with stallions

He animates the inanimate
Gives sight through Braille
He rises and falls
To the cunning of mind
Conquering everything
Except himself

Book Two

Transcended

*My hungry searching for God
has awakened the core of my being
and revealed God to me in ways
I could've never imagined
thus, creating a relationship only obtainable
through this divine affair*

December 24

It's official
The Messiah of whom
The prophets wrote
Is coming to earth
The hope of glory

The stage has been set
There's no turning back
But there will be hell to pay
Before he finishes the task

His birth papers
Have been authorized
Legions of angels
Have secured the skies
Gabriel
Sinclair
And Michael will lead

Their armies arrayed
For spiritual warfare

There can be no error
No interruption of plan
God will perform
His desire for man

Divine has inhabited
The womb of a virgin
One umbilical cord
Connects earth to heaven

Let there be no slips
No ransom demands
God has become
The substitute for man

The story of his coming
Will make headlines
Shepherds will announce
His coming with song

The blind will now see
Who the scriptures
Have hidden
Until the fullness of time
He was cloaked in enigma

Wise men will seek him
Children will adore him
Shepherds will bow
Prostrate before him
Heathens will rage
Demons will tremble
Nations will reject
The salvation he brings them

A two-edged
Will spring from his mouth
His tongue shall be
A devouring fire

In the power of a command
He'll raise the dead
Turn the tides of rivers
Defy the laws of nature

Lazarus, come forth
Peace, be still
Woman thou art loosed
Daughter, be healed
Pick up your bed
Rise up and walk

He without sin
Cast the first stone

Diviners will report
His birth a miracle
Scholars will note
He's the world's greatest healer
Claiming to be God
The most reverenced above idols
The most controversial
Of all human encounters

But he must be stopped
The night before Christmas
If we snatch him from the womb
There will be no resurrection

No festive dancing
Across the rivers he bore
When he spoke from the vortex
Dividing the waters
After his crucifixion
He'll be declared a martyr
Interest in his life
Will only grow stronger

Libraries will not be able
To contain his story
That his Father will manifest
To his glory
No volume
No data base
No www.com
Can contain the legacy
Of almighty God

King of kings
Lord of lords
Prince of peace
Savior of all

His Name exalted
Above the throne
Wonderful
Counselor
Everlasting Father

The conspiracy against him
Will have no might to conquer
Hated for his claims
Despised for his power

So to protect our interest
And assure our victory
The most decorated generals
Have already been commissioned

Barring any unforeseen
Interference
King Herod has planned
The killing of Jesus

Three kings
Lead the way
Even if he makes it here
His death warrant
Has already been sealed

Wait a minute...
Did I command noise
Then what's that rumbling
Through the spirit realm

Heaven and earth
Tilt and shake
The universe of galaxies
Make way for his descent

The noise barrier is shattering
We're losing our balance
Those who share my dream
The plan is unraveling!!!!

Hush...
I hear them singing
Joy to the World
The Lord has come

There is no speech
Nor language
Where his voice
Is not heard

The light of angels
Has encircled the world
Let earth receive her King

It's back to defeated
To remap our strategy
He's on his way now
To manifest destiny

But there'll be other mistakes
Before he says "It's Finished"

Mary and Joseph
Can't protect him
Forever

Children have accidents
Get lost in the crowd
The Marketplace
The Synagogue
The Feast of Tabernacles

Remember
They're other children
Besides
Their "Darling Little Jesus"
Who they've made Lord
Overall his other siblings

But he's as much human now
As he is divine
So there's still a chance
To turn things around

Hold on
Don't abandon your confidence
In the plan we've devised
His steps will be numerous
But his days are divided

I'll put hatred in the heart
Of an entire community
He'll be isolated
With only family to befriend him

No child can survive
The disdain of men
If that doesn't work
I've still got a plan

Remember he's a stranger
Who walks and talks
In a foreign language

The earthly life
Will be too much too endure
He'll long for his Father
And his heavenly kingdom

The Pharisees will mock him
The Sadducees will sneer
The Sanhedrin will follow him
Resolutely
Year after year

As he grows in statue
And uncommon wisdom
He will boldly assert
Himself a deity
That God is his Father
And he the Son
That he and the Father
Bear witness as one

In the Wilderness of Judea
I will challenge his claim
If thou be the Son of God
Make bread from this stone

Fall down
Worship at my feet
And this grandiose folly
Shall be your gift from me

Cast yourself headlong
From the pinnacle
Of the temple
If you're the Son of God
Surely He will help you

Doris Wellington

We'll be there
With the woman
At the well
And on the roadside
Begging
Through blind Bartimaeus

At the tomb of Lazarus
In the house of Bethany
At the pool of Bethesda
In the Synagogue
On the Sabbath

In the boat
With his disciples
Amongst the multitudes
Seeking healing
Taunting the woman
Healed from her issue

Did I say healed
As in we lost her
She refused to turn back
Without touching his garment

Thirteen years of scheming
Down the drain
Because she found the answer
Calling His Name

But we're on it
The feast of the Passover
Will avail us opportunity
The magistrates are already
Preparing his funeral

He'll show up
Full of himself
Proclaiming his existence
Before Abraham
I Am this
I Am that
Bread of heaven
Water that quenches

The true vine
The good shepherd
The tree of life
I am the way
The truth
And life

Well the powers
Have conspired
To shut him down
A cross spectrum
Of his enemies
Have become one voice

"Crying
This man blasphemes
Saying he is God
The Messiah
Who the prophets
Have prophesied

Alpha and Omega
Beginning
And End

Who has come
In the power and
Authority of infinity

I'll destroy this temple
And in three days
Rebuild it
Then
I'll come again
To claim my Kingdom

You don't take my life
I freely give it
To fulfill the will
Of my Father in Heaven
For those who wait
For the promise of the Spirit
I'll baptize in my body

One people in unity

But...
To prove the Holy writ
Is subject to error
We will birth deception
In the heart of Judas

He'll betray his Master
For thirty pieces of silver
Peter will deny him
The rest will scatter

Pontius Pilate
Will choose Barabbas
Then wash his hands
Forsaking justice
For the politics of men

Crucify him
Cast lots for his garment
Mock him
Spit on him
Put the cross
On his shoulders
Flog him
Spear him
Until the blood
Cries out
In anguish

Until the spikes
In his body
Cut off his circulation

Bind him
With curses
Blind his eyes
Until he
Regurgitates
The claim
That he's one with God

Greater than the scrolls
That bind our souls to wait
For the Messianic promise
Of which
The scriptures speak

Tighten his head
About with thorns
Until he laments
The day he was ever born
"Eli Eli la'ma sabach'thani"

Hang him between
Two worthless sinners
Lest he forgets
He's a man to be pitied

Threatening to dismantle
The life of the rich
Cleansing the lepers
Healing the sick

Raising the dead
Keeping company
With whores
Reversing the curse
Lifting the sword

Breaking the chains
And bonds of the wicked
Commanding the wind
Casting out demons

In no uncertain
Terms
Silence him
Until he's nothing more
Than a dead man forgotten

Hang "King of the Jews"
Over his head
So those who follow him
Will grieve his death

Doris Wellington

A spectacle of characters
Will gather to witness
What will become
Of their model citizen

Pontius Pilate
The Roman soldiers
Mothers
And fathers
Sisters and brothers

The scribes
The Pharisees
The chief priests
And elders
The women who
Served him
Weeping and wailing

The lad whose lunch
Fed five thousand
The centurion's servant
Jairus daughter

Pilate's wife
Mary Magdalene
The woman who poured
Alabaster
On his feet

The governor
The pontiff
The court jesters
And Jews

Caiaphas
The High Priest
John the Beloved
Kings and Queens

Blurred
Faces
Obscured by the crowd
Voices muted
By the passion
Of Christ

Reconciling
Redeeming
With every drop of blood

Surrender
Transformed
Unconditional
Love

Words once veiled
Thrust into the light
The heavens bowed
In blackness
The earth lost its balance

For three divine hours
He held creation captive
Pouring his fullness
To fulfill the world's hunger

Enduring
The agony of the cross
He forgave our ignorance
Father forgive them
They know not
What they're doing

In the midst
Of rancor
And
Nature's reviling
A thief
Condemned
Receives
Divine pardon
The moment
He believed

His death sentence
Commuted
Blood covered
His past
And gave
Promise for the future

"Today
You shall be with me
In paradise"

Drawn from the bowels
Of a woman's travail
The mother who birthed him
The woman at the well

Elizabeth
Anna
Mary and Martha
The widow of Nan
The Syrophoenician
Woman
Woman, behold your son
"Brother"
Behold your mother

The water that quenched
The thirst of nations
The house that built me
The wheel that shaped me

The womb that thrust me
Into my purpose
The altar that held
My destiny in trust

Chosen by God
Favored among women
The faith that believed
I was sent to save her

"Father into your hands
I commit my spirit

Then he bowed his head
And declared
"It's finished"

The heathen
Raged
The abyss
Trembled
The blood
Washed away
The middle wall of petition

The veil of the temple
Was rent in twain
The tabernacle of God
Is now with man

We have his treasure
In earthen vessels
Our sentence
Reversed
Our inheritance
Reclaimed
Even the Roman
Soldier
Had to confess
Surely this man
Was the Son of God

In a few short hours
He took hell by force
Made an open show
By death on the cross

Stormed the enemy's camp
Took captivity captive
While legions stood by
Dumbfounded
And helpless

Conquered
In a moment
Death
Hell
And the grave

Then
The first day of the week
He rose again

Tell me who can
Stand before us
When we call
On that great Name
Immutable
Infallible
Invictus
Jesus

Through
Two-thousand years
His victory
Challenged
By everyone
And everything
Demonically
Possible

Heretics
False prophets
Agnostics
Atheists
Hirelings
Idolaters
Renouncing the faith

Apostates
Demagogues
Worshippers
Skeptics
Wolves
In sheep's clothing
Mockers and haters

Still
He lives
Every conspiracy thwarted
The Christmas miracle
Still the gift of the Father

He lives
His will be done
Joy to the world
The Lord has come

Christmas Eve

My breathing flows
To an even tempo
Of silence
Hugged by the warmth
Of the December sun
I lie quiet in the embrace
Of living

Still
Rains my thoughts
I'm enraptured
In a current of memories
Of Christmases gone pass

So I pause
To pay tribute
To the Giver
Who came

And comes
But does not disappoint

No elves make ready his journey
No horsemen drive the chariot
There is no sleigh
Or reindeers
Not even Rudolph
Has been summoned

He brings one gift
The whole world will share
One promise
Bound
In human flesh

A virgin
No man had ever touched
Unites heaven and earth
In birth

A baby born to captive hearts
Declared by prophets
Feared by kings
The wise still seek his counsel
Still hail him
Prince of Peace

Worshipped by shepherds
Adored by children
He came
Hope glorious
For the solemn
Faith for the faithless
Life water
For the desolate

Blood to bind nations
Bread to reverse
The famish of spirit
Seed for the barren

He came
Fruit
For the Sower
Light

Piercing the unknown
Conspicuous
But not discerned
Hidden
But fully exposed

He came
Oil
To anoint Kings
Kings
To dethrone
To conceal truth
He came
Truth
To dismantle fables

Parables
To deny the wise and prudent
Access
To the righteousness
They refused

He came
Grace
To teach forgiveness
Love
To shatter hate
Salvation
To condemn sin
In full
To anchor the soul

Fragmented
Disjointed
Predisposed
To failure
And wretchedness

He came
Humbly bold
To defy arrogance
One
To resist being cloned
A full fountain
To fill empty souls

He came
A weapon
To disarm evil
Love
To redeem fear
And set its captives free
He came
He conquered
He reigns

Joy to the world
The Lord has come

Surrender

God
You got mail
I googled your origin
But it couldn't be found
Science says you're a phony
No birth certificate
Confirms your claim to eternity
Your deity is questionable
Your work
Speculative
No one who ever lived
Witnessed your coming

Out of vortex of a mystery
You came
Bearing the record of
An unsubstantiated history
One time I pondered you
Long and hard
I almost fell off into the unknown

An endless curiosity
That yielded no knowledge
Gripped me with fear
Left me appalled
Questions hovered
In the vortex of silence
And returned to me void
Empty
Yet full
Dark
Yet lighted
Quiet
Yet deafening to the ear

The eye of infinity
Piercing the ear
Of the mortal
Human
Seeking access
To a realm off limit
No access
No authority to enter
No divinity code

Just curiosity
The lust to know
Probing the boundaries
Of what can't be seen
Hidden realities
Fantasies
And dreams

God-seeking
For all the wrong reasons
No God fear
Just a quest of pride
Longing to build
Man castles in the sky
Hoping against hope
That You will be their neighbor
No accountability for wrong
No penalties for evil
Relegated
To a god-man
No lesser
No greater
Just one lives high
The other lives lower

No heaven
No hell
No sin
Or salvation
Just another layer
To an inflated ego

So
There I was
On the ledge of apprehension
Nowhere to move forward
No way to end it

Father
Forgive
Return me to me
The hidden consumes me
Mortifies my reasoning
I'm about to be swept up
In eternal ignorance
Where all options closes
To the portal of mortality
The ways of the previous
Would no longer exist

I would simply be a blur
In an invisible spectrum
No one would ever
Trace my footsteps
Or trajectory
My genealogy
Would be altered forever
Lost in a space
That not even science
Would discover

So I surrender
I repent
I might not have the answer
But I know longer question
Your existence

Let the brave inquire
Let the fools contest
Let those who seek to be god
Hold on to their science

I've been there
Searching mystery and lore
On the precipice of insanity
Falling headlong
Into the abyss
Or being pulled upward
Into a vastness
I cannot define

Lower me I pray
Let my feet touch the familiar
If I never understand
I'll be satisfied believing
That beyond this gated place
Of the material and tangible
Lies a chasm

That one must be invited to explore
Or die never knowing
What lies beyond
The mystic realm
Of here and there

Save me I pray
From asking
I have no desire to know

Feed me what you desire
But lead m in the quiet
Quest of knowledge
That does not infringe upon
Offend
Or assault
Your integrity

For If I knew
If we knew
If we could comprehend
The mystique of the majestic
We would all be God
And undoubtedly
We would war
Each other for the title
No one wanting to settle

Lordship would be auctioned
To the highest bidder
Angels would be slaves
To the whims of mere humans
So herein again
I acknowledge my submission
Whether real
Surreal
Myth
Or fantasy

I believe
In God....
(.)

Flight of the Trumpeter Swan

Father
Journey with me
To the center of my world
Where every day conscious
I seek to share your voice

In the marketplace
With those known to me
And with strangers

There has been no void
Of words
Since I determined flight
My pen
Binds my heart to worlds
Transforms my reality
From norm
To endless possibilities
Opening doors that do not revolve
But is the portal that connects
Mortal to immortality

Encounters
Of unordinary mystique
From coast to coast
I traverse
Alone with my thoughts
To guide me

Engorging magnificence
That only a master
Can interpret

The euphoric splendor
And serenity
In the shires of Europe
The romanticism
Of France
The nomadic plains
And rustic paths
Of the Netherlands

The spiritual
Awakening of the Tibetan
Experience
The aloneness
And self-indulgence
Of the ever winding
Everglades

Populated by species
Of another form

I see it all
Sense its awe
Through the simplistic art
Of bibliography

There is nothing that rivals
The subtext of thoughts
Transcribed
Onto canvases
Of curious origin
Recycled and
Reincarnated
Between times

Grocery bags
Toilet tissue
Napkins
Scraps of discarded
Matter
Like labels
From the neckline of
A fresh cotton cheongsam

Or bell bottom trousers

The back cover
Of the King James Bible
Or envelopes
That hold antiquities
A fresh word
Revives it
And gives it new meaning

Thoughts fleeting
Like a slideshow
Are hurriedly captured
Archived on the flap of a cereal box
Or the inside cover
Of a First Edition
Prophesying
My expectation
And Holds my dreams
In trust

Those who thought me dead
Or thought to will me so
Have all but repented

My social network
Enlarges
Then diminishes
To foil the efforts
Of those who follow
Me to drink
From wells they did not plant
Or doubted existed

While my musing races
Ahead of me
And I stand
Amongst the eminent
Of ancient wonders

People
Places
And things
Unforgettable

The pyramids
Indigenous to Africa
The sand dunes
Of the Nile
The meandering lure
Of the Niger
Beguiled
By its mysticism and magic

We (my pen and I)
Have made a covenant
Where there is no wonder
We will create it

Line upon line
Precept upon precept
Here a little
There a little
Doodling
And dabbling
Until
Out of the amorphous
Genius is formed

And both observer and
Participate
Are enraptured by idioms
And axioms
Grafted and
Extrapolated
From eras and annals
Revisited
Edited
Deleted and
Reborn

To fit no certain criteria
Except to grant
The power to transcend times
And spaces
With the broad or narrow
Brush
Of perspective

Animating the inanimate
Humanizing nature
Giving voice to creatures
Of the most humbling sort
A frog becomes a prince
Man takes the form of beast
An ant becomes a giant
Woman converses with tree
Beauty is distorted by rivalry
Fantasy is pursued like gold

Life is unraveled by pain
Pleasure is the law
Of the soul

Angels walk as humans
In the realm of mortal failure
And humans take wings
And soar into the heavenly
Defying gravity
To escape their pretentious utopia

The canvas enlarges itself
With liberties forbidden
By the conventional diktat
Of sanity
Blue becomes melancholy
And madness
Polarized
By non-existing realities

Red is the temptress
That lures to despairing
White is the innocence
Of children
Black is the night that bids
Them solace
With iambic
Restraints
Or limericks
Of yore

I am a candidate
Feed my famine
To feasting
Upon the fatness of labor
Temper
But do not upbraid
My ravenous folly
Starved from mediocrity
Thirsting for the zenith
Of transformation

Today
This January
Two-thousand twelve
My hunger is singular
To soar upon words
Yanked from pages
Of documents
Saved in cryptic files
On computer devices
Or the flash drives
External hard drives
And other places tucked
Naked in memory

All things considered
Where my dreams are
Concerned
I believe the time has come
To emerge from the shadows
Of the understudy
And the apprentice

And take my position
In the universe
As prophet
Possessing the tablets
Years born
In isolation

I speak to every page
Written in secret
Every word
Birthed in frustration
And burning passion
To change the world
I declare a place
Of prominence
Among scholars
And readers of letters
Among those less likely
To care one way or the other
Dreams
Take wings and fly
Do not pull back
Not even for me
Make your own path
Claim your own place

Do not move over
To accommodate critics
Build it
And we will come

In a world indulged with imposters
Become the life force
That propels my journey
To testimonials
Possessed by those
Who overcome

Take wings and fly
To the outer layers
Of the hemisphere
To the inner core
Of nations who sit
In shallow feasts

Delight the heart
Of children
Empower the soul of women
Make her story count

The veiled and the unveiled
The married
And the single
The poverty stifled
And the opulent
Whatever her field of labor

Sing songs
That herald her greatness
Her claim to power
Her triumph over tragedy
The karma
That marked her descent
Into depravity

Whether prostitute
Or madam
Born again
Or heathen
Trustworthy
Or cunning
Preposterous
Or believable
Peninnah
Or Hannah
Jezebel
Or Miriam

Whether the color is purple
Or no color at all
Whether the daughters
Of the bond
Or children of the free

Lift up their void
Like a trumpet
Speak their names
Until tombstones
Rewrite their epitaphs

Until warriors
Thought dead
Regurgitate indifference
Spew the venom
Of apathetic living
Upon those
Who quit prematurely

Partner with the weak
Dance
With the disadvantaged
Enlighten the ignorant
Tease the wise and prudent
Honor those deserving
Teach those
Without learning

Light the path of the spirit
Indulge the heart of lovers
Feast with those famished
Withhold the bread of gluttony
Sing merry songs
To the sorrowful
Inspire healing for the afflicted

Give and it shall be given
In multiplied portions
Of praise

Fill the wells of drought
And desolation
Tear down the walls of hatred
Build bridges
That unite the world
In laughter
Build castles
For angels on sabbatical

Inspire fathers to return
To children abandoned
Encourage the widows
To channel pain
Into purpose
Call mothers back
From riotous living
And neglect of children

Stir controversy
Among the truthless
And those at ease in Zion
Indulge the mind
With literary verbosity
Metaphors
And allegories
That bridge the real with surrealism

Dreams
Take wings...
I Command you to fly...
In the midst
Of deadness
And fallow grounds

Fly
Where the realist
Dare trample
Where the souls of feet
Thirst from weariness
Fly
Reawaken the parched
And dry places
Call the birds back
From migration
The winter is past
Springtime beckons
Song

And when you've done
All you can
Stand
In awe
Of God

January's Prayer
Lie me down
And get me up
In thee O'Lord
I put my trust
I shall not die
Before I wake
For in thee O'Lord
Is your promise safe
I put my trust in you alone
I cannot exit
Until I'm done
The latter rain
Overpowering
The former
The answer racing
To overtake the promise
Favor so profuse
I must trust forward
The harvest gushes forth
Before born

future etched
In your mind
Nothing can impeach my time
From every direction

I hear a mighty wind
Pushing
Pulling
Screaming
Yelling
Daughter of God
It's your time
To fly

February 11

Tribute to Whitney
Today I heard
Whitney passed
The Voice'
Unsurpassed
And
Incomparable
Beautiful
Statuesque
Contagious aura
Now lies dead
In human form
Whatever her demons
Whatever her challenge
The Whitney God loaned us
Is done with that battle
It doesn't matter now
How she finished
There's no redo
No editing
No cutting away
For a more flattering
Image

We couldn't airbrush
Her final hours
Before she slipped away
Prematurely
Life force still hovering
For an encore
That will never
Be given
By bowing

No cheering
No flowers thrown
At the feet
Of ardent fans
Screaming for more
"Whitney, we love you
Whitney, you're the greatest
She just whispered into the air
Yes, Jesus loves me
For the Bible tells me so

No technical score
No mixing board
No backup singers
Of course
She never needed them

Her voice so mammoth
She could carry any range

Doris Wellington

Reverberating
Across time zones
Snatching endurance
From the wind
Breaking sound barriers
Holding a note captive
With unadulterated skill

Blazing trails
Knocking down walls
What a treasure
What a delight to consume

Immeasurable depth
Not soon forgotten
My mind besieged
With wondering
My voice choke
The tears wouldn't hold
Is she really dead?

I hold my breath
As words flow
Through my hope
Turn on the news
It's all there
I resign myself
Yield to the truth
Whitney is gone

Just yesterday
I removed the Jet
With her picture
On the cover
Beneath one
Bearing the face
Of another
And whispered
"Whitney,
You had your day"
Only to suggest
That while she slept
Others prepared
To take their place
In the spotlight

She broke down barriers
With her gift
Went where black women
Had never been before
Whether through the lens
Or behind a mic
She had the most
Extraordinary voice
I'd ever encountered

Powerful
Profound
Tour de force
Twentieth Century
Renaissance

She bellowed our anthem
Until men in arms
Lifted their eyes
To salute her God
Our Father
Which art in heaven
Hallowed be
Thou liberty
Of thee we sing
Even when
Less than sober
She fell short
He was still Holy
King of Kings
Lord of Lords

Raised I believe
To serve the Lord
She renounced Him
In the life she chose
With a hundred million dollars
To indulge herself

Consorting with danger
She tempted the devil

Alcohol
Smokes, crack
And sex
Everything available
In excess

I search my journals
To find marked the places
Where I bore her burden
In fasting and praying
In the thirteenth year
From the day I began
She abdicates the life
God had freely given

I combed journals
Searched the deep places
Of the mind
Back and forward
To and fro
For the ledgers of prayers
When I lifted her to God

In visitations
And dreams
Shaven
Exposed
Dead children lying
In a watery womb
Veiled in black
Standing on the podium
Reaching
Missing
The hem of His garment
Then back and forth
Walking amiss
Through the same valley
Of the shadow of death

Dream after dream
I called out her name
"Whitney Houston,"
I command you to live
You have everything
Don't chase the fantasy
It is but the illusion
Of your reality
Illusive
Fleeting
A sounding brass
And a tinkling cymbal
A cunning slight
That can never compete
With Jesus Christ

She stopped
And turned a glance
I saw the bleeding
In her heart
So gently I carried her
To a place of rest
Angels went before me
To guard my words
Or she would have been gone
Long before

In the beginning
Of the thirteenth year
Since the day
I conceived and carried
In the garment of prayer
Father, I sacrifice
This day of eating
For the fruit of deliverance
For my sister, Whitney

Her spiritual life and
Confession of Christ
Wavering
To perform
Her desire for flesh
Her desecration
Of the covenant of marriage

Substance abuse
And destructive habits
Balance in sexuality
Confusion of mind
Emotions
And action

Deliver her
From
Self-destructive patterns
That she might live
Divinely aware
Possessed by gratitude
For the gift she possesses
Baptize her
In the Holy Spirit
And speak in tongues
As you give utterance

That the voice
Of the true prophet
Will manifest in her life
To set in order
Truth from lies
Friend from foe
Real from fantasy
Weak from strong

Paraphrased from Journal #28a (Pages 120-146)

And as in some reports
I heard
Whitney Houston
Spoke in tongues
In Houston Texas
With her longtime friend
She had the visitation
That mirrored my prayers

She collapsed in praise
Before God and man
She held her soul up to
God again
She poured dry her tears
Into his arms
Here am I
Nothing more than broken
Heart bleeding
Gift emasculated
Sanctify me
One more time
Then take me into
Your eternity

No foul play
Just no resistance
She renounced her demons

Repented of her sins
Forgive me, Lord
For my sin
My gift bereft
My life in ruins
What have I wrought
To my daughter's scorn

She never heard
Me weep for her
She never saw my tears
She never knew I carried her
She never knew I cared
Never witnessed

My phone call to Pebbles
Trying the best way
I knew to tell her
Whitney
Turn
Before it's too late

You're valued
And accepted
By the God of all grace

And now you know
Even also as you are known
The Lord did love you
But you loved the world more

We all wanted
We all yearned
To hear you belt it

Just one more gin
So now you see
What was hidden
The faces of those
Who carried your burden

Today
The true prophet spoke
Whitney,
You've sang your swan song
Follow your angel
It's time to come home

February 16

Today we mourned
A national treasure
In the personality
Of Whitney Houston

Pop Princess
Drop dead beauty
Model statuesque
Vocals to die for
Unsurpassed talent
Unrivalled charisma
Today we celebrate
A supernova

Dominating the charts
Invoking envy
Vexed by her own life force
Awarded for her brilliance
Flags lowered
To half-staff position

Nations stood still
Four hours for Whitney
Statesmen
Friends
Family
And industry

Today the world
Sent home
Its prodigal princess
She slipped away
Her voice now muted
Behind the travail
Of those who prayed

Her place left hollow
Friends cling
To the last syllable
Of her last conversation
The world serenade
Their pop diva
With straining vocals
Of one or another
Of her classic songs
The signature sound
We will always remember
The contagious smile
Elegance
Unrivalled
By any
This century

Self-assured
And confident appearing
Until the lights are raised
And thousands stare
Hauntingly into her presence

She was after all
Every woman
Marrying for love

Loving her man
Blessing family
Supporting friends
Wrapped and warped
In ambiguity
Strong
But weak
Bold
But afraid
Beautiful
But at times
Feeling less than
Accomplished
Yet not fully aware
Of the power given
Rising
Falling
Between two worlds
Rich
Carrying the baggage of the poor
Walking along the edge
Of Jesus Christ
Making a mess
Of a perfectly good life

Troubled marriages
Disgruntled friends
Jealousy
Rivalry
Discontentment

A merry-go-round
Of self-destruction
A loss of love
For her number one fan
Whitney Houston
Stopped loving herself

Everyday
A light awakens
For its earth journey
Another fades
Behind the reckless
Disregard
Of the darkness
That surrounds
And stalks
The brilliance
Of all those earthborn
With the mantle
To change this world
For better

If we could first
But conquer us
The stalking of demons
The gates of hell
The temptation
To bow to flesh
And blood
Happiness in a pill

Contentment in a bottle
Character auctioned
To the highest bidder
No where to store
The excess of pleasure
Until grace withdraws
The promise of tomorrow
The whispering echo of the spirit
I've fallen
This time…
I can't get up
Still
We will always remember

February 21

Today we stood
One prayer lifted
One faith bowed
In steadfast resistance
An apostle
A pastor
A prophet in the fire
Three cords intertwined
To make one cry
We bind any threat
Against your daughter

February 27

This morning
The vortex whispered
Every time a star is born
Creation stands in wonder
Piercing light
Applause of thunder
Robed in supernatural
Splendor
Is strategically
Prepared
For its earth journey

Parents are chosen
From the book of names
Then scratched over
Because of rebellion
And self-addicted ways
Of human beings
Who though
Sent by God
Are born by man
Takes destiny
Into their own hands
To ruin or raise
To the place of power
That God has marked
For
Everyday a star is born

March 5, 2012

Today I heard
Lies being shaped
For deception
To be spewed
Into the atmosphere
To create the delusion
Of truth
Though
There is no truth
In it really
It is being
Masterfully package
For human conception

The faint of heart
Those disillusioned
Wounded soldiers
On sabbatical from truth
Backsliders
Weak minded
Those driven about
By every
Wind and doctrine
Silly women
Arrogant
Those ever reaching
But never grasping

Whose made idols
Of their own voices
Who rather believe the lie
Because truth
Sets every soul
Free from captive
Exposes
Imposters
Quacks
And charlatans
And pirates
Who pillage the vaults
Of heirs
And heiresses

Today
That imposter
Showed his plan
Marginalize
Christianity
By deleting
All references
In the Holy Bible
That Jesus Christ
Is the Son of God
Under mind the gospel
By spewing heresy
Create reasonable doubt
In the mind of believers
Make religion
A unilateral project

No one deity
Can claim sovereignty
Let's just merge Christianity
And Islam
Meet on common ground
Call it Chrislam
Stop swatting gnats
And swallowing camels

March 4

Mark the day
Place a ribbon around the time
When I stood
Alone at a podium
Except for God
He held me close
Retrained my heart
From the fear of faces
Staring long into my eyes
Youth exposed
To prolonged silence
They don't know me
I don't know them
Their reservations and mine
Wrestle in the atmosphere
One will hold the other captive
Until the wrestling ceases
And one capitulates
In defeat

Who will it be?
I'm certain not me
They say the same
So I ventured past the line of dare
Taking the lead
In a narrative that unfolds
In metaphors
And allegories
Across the chasm of time
Still relevant
Still the greatest story
Ever told

March 10, 2012

This morning I cried
In the presence of God
Father I just
Want do your will
When was the last time
I had a vision

Came
"You just did
Embrace it
'I'm Here

April 9, 2012—To Rome with Love

Today I was scheduled to go to Rome
My ticket pressed on the inside of baggage
Waiting at the door
The cry of a stranger
The love of a friend
Calls
And I must answer
Her heart has gone weary
The mind wrestles against itself
The body famished of hope
Wonders between panic and stress

There are no comforting faces
They are all her enemies
Swine who wait to devour her flesh
To cast their net
And dispossess her sanity
The voices beckons
And she cannot know from where
As haunting as the night is black
They stalk her for prey
She cannot rest
They are everywhere

On the train from Sicily
In the center of Rome
They fill the Coliseum
They hide behind the ancient statue
Mocking her disarm
She is alone
Except for God
But where is he
Has he abandoned her quest
Her yielded soul
To his work

She came for him
He sent for her
She heard his voice
As clearly as she has ever
Heard him
Calling her from the busyness of home
To move in uncertain faith
To walk on water
To calm raging seas
To vanquish demons to hell
To set the weary at rest

Where is he
Here in this great antiquity
Where the disciples once walked
The cobblestone streets
And the relics of Rome

Where is the man
Who came with her from ~America~
Only to abandon her dream
Soul unwilling to follow
The spirit's feast
Hungry
But not enough to eat
Weary of monotony
But not enough to seek
Disenchanted with mediocrity
But not enough to pursue greatness

Left her alone with the lions
Alone with abandonment
As her pillow
Alone to ponder ~God
And his purpose
Walking ...
Drifting...
Hoping
Tired ..
But not enough to die...

So a phone call
Answers a prayer for help
And midwives prepare
For an intervention

Who shall we send
And who shall go for us
And I answered
Here am I
Lord
Send me...

And so the journey began
Speaking to her by phone
Calling those things forth
From the mind of ~God
Hurling a word into her path
Commanding her to hold on

There's a word coming
On the wings of faith
Flowing across the waters
To plant your feet
On the solid rock
The trip was ticketed in my name
From April 9 through the 17
Mission
Snatch her from the grips
Of Rome
Bring God's child
Safely home

I hugged her doubting
With prayer
If you don't give up
We won't despair
Just one day prior to my leaving
A message on Sunday morning
Courage had overcome
The hopeless
Had taken strength
And boarded a plane
And was now safely
In Philadelphia again
My bags still packed
My ticket still good
The mission accomplished
The enemy confused
As always
God has prevailed
In Jesus Name
The word spoken to a desolate place
Has birth deliverance

May 30, 2012

Today I listened with my left ear
I hear the serenade of birds
The roar of an ignition
The hum of an engine

Two women converse with nature
There are no squirrels
I hear one say
A man scolds a child

Come back here
Get off that curb
A radio blasts a rapper
The car bounces

The speakers vibrate
The two women sound their disgust
My left ear giggles
The things the ear hears

The voices go mute
To the background of
The wind rustling through
 The leaves of spring

A door slams
The hinge of the gate
Locks
A dog barks a command

That no one can interpret
Except in dog codes
Which I do not understand
And do not care to know

The things of which dogs
Speak
Footsteps scrap the sidewalk
A man's
A child's
Silenced by the sudden clanking
Of a lawn mower
In need of oil

Not the fine oils of the Himalayas
Just motor oil
To calm its unbalanced toil

I cover my right ear
To test the depth and distance
Of sound in my left
A car door slams
Familiar voice
Moving towards the gate

The alarm on the cellular
Sinks into the pit of my ear
Its 8:30am
I rise to hush its monotony

The doorbell chimes
And the two women
Emerges accompanied by
Two demanding toddlers

In their high pitched
Feverish tones
Telling their mothers
What they want
And do not want to do

This is all happening
As pots are placed on a stove
Downstairs
Water runs from a faucet
And one of the women
Have a brief conversation
With another woman
In the house
Her mother

My phone is ringing to the music
Of Scott Joplin
I answer
My voice is still
Morning heavy

Feet that could only
Belong to a maniac
Race downstairs
Two steps at a time
The organ blasts
The drums rumble
The keyboard is being teased

The sounds of pending rain
Announcing itself
Through the thrust of nature
Bending the branches of trees

Whispers of water
Tap against the windowsill
The blinds clang
The curtain flutter in sync
With organ keys

Gospel songs from an iPhone
Identifying the caller

And all my hopes of a quiet
Morning are dashed
By the welcomed blessing
Of hearing in my left ear

Though I knew it existed
I defy any word hovering
To the contrary
The ringing
The throbbing
The chiming
The sound of squirting
The subtle stabs of pain
Are but symptoms

Of a condition already healed
By the blood of Jesus
Thank God for hearing

May 31, 2012

Last night I heard a child pray
A girl of three led the way
She placed her hand across my
Chest
In childlike faith, she confessed
Jesus is Lord

In the name of Jesus
In redundant monotony
No one dared
Stop her

Her tiny, fisted hands raised
Her fragile feet stomping
Glory
In the name of Jesus
Redundant fury
For the enemy

A child
Empowered to lead
No fear of rejection
Or grammatical errors
No pride of spirit
Innocent to a fault

No quenching
The Spirit

Head lifted as high as
A 3-year-old could lift it
Advancing God a praise
For miracles
Still invisible
In the womb of heaven

Thank you Jesus
She boldly declared
Face twisted
And perplexed
Of the unknown
In that moment
Being unfolded
 As we watched
In awesome wonder

One by one
She drew us
Into her ministry
Relentless
She continued
Until she had laid
Her sinless palms
Upon the body
Of all their present

Minutes
Appeared like hours passing
Before the child
Drunk and inhabited
Staggered from our midst
Still speaking
Still declaring
The name of Jesus

The car was opened
She was placed
Gently into her seat
And belted for safety
I still hear the echo
Of her faith
Clinging to the chill
Of the Spring night

Everything within me
Bore witness
This was no ordinary
Gathering
This was divine
Meeting humans yielded
Pouring into unsuspecting
Vessels
The pure oil of the anointing
Summoned
By the least likely

Rendering flesh impotent
Knowledge void
Reinforcing scriptures
Where Christ confers
His approval
Upon innocence
Except ye come as
Little children
Unpretentious
Without hypocrisy
You cannot
Enter
The presence of God

I bowed my head
In reverence
Thanking God
The Holy Spirit
For reminding us
In the simplest way
Possible
How to get his attention

Without the fanfare
Of religion
Or the boasting of
Credentials
Casting our pearls
Before swine

Or pouring new oil
In empty vessels
Or whitewashed sepulchers
Carrying dead men's
Sins

Father I bowed
To the visitation
Of your Spirit
Whatever He brings
I humbly receive your miracle
Through the prayers
Of a child
Crying out amongst us
Lord
I surrender
To the healing
Birthed through her

Two ultrasounds proved
That you heard her
As she offered her prayer
The purest
Among us
Whatever the mammogram
Revealed
Was but another opportunity
To summon
The power of faith

And she did

June 23, 2012

The Widow of Zarephath

Today I lift myself in worship
In an offering of tears
And prayer
I cannot utter
Words run together
And appear muffled
In a mingling
Of unfamiliar sounds

Why do I feel alone
When I know
You're with me
My heart feels heavy
Though I testify freedom

There are no fetters
Around my will
No chains
Around my soul

Still
There are answers
That elude me
And questions
That beckons me, pause

Can one
Ever really know
The journey
Of the soul

Are we ever really free
In this life
 Toilsome
Burdened
Desiring what
We cannot be
Filled with
Restless worries

June 25, 2012

Today I wake
To my mother's prayers
Lord, I declare

This woman doesn't quit.
The phone rings
She answers in her grogginess
Words still trapped
In the oblivion of sleep

The partner begins
She finishes
Calling out the names
Of Children
I listen for mine

Doris Wellington

And amidst the declarations
I hear her say
Remember Doris
Her family in Milwaukee
Keep Her
Strengthen her
Heal her body

Give her the desires of her heart
Only you know
What she prays in secret
I pull the warm covers
Around my face

The prayers go mute
Behind the hum
Of the air conditioner
And I drift back to sleep
Contemplating
What faith
What awesome endurance

Ying and yang
And karma stand still
The earth revolves
The heavens opens to reveal
Reciprocity

The seedtime and harvest
Of a woman's prayers
All is not perfect
In her world
Of 81 years

There are specks of crumbs
In the carpet
A coat of dust
On the dresser
Old, dried condiments
In the frig

The cabinets needs cleaning
The baths needs scrubbing
The laundry needs a ring
In the old sturdy washer

And from what I can tell
The walls could stand
A little elbow muscle
But in all of that

Room for improvement
There's one thing
For certain
The prayers are

A constant
In season and out
Alone
In the absence
Of applause

Or the presence of company
The supplicant
Arises
To an internal clock

The invitation
Awakens the dead sleeping
And pulls them into
A dance on the altar

She answers
Here I am Lord
Send me
The dishes can wait
The chores will be there

When the last petition
Is made
Call me Lord
And I will answer
Teach me your way
And I will teach others
To pray

To intercept justice
And plead for grace
She stands
In agreement

With the word
That formed worlds
There is no compromise
No negotiation
She speaks
And heaven listens
And releases her answer

The prince of the air
Will align against her
Conspire to steal
What her faith has birth

And there will be a rumble
In the heavenly realm
Angels will guard
What the demons can't have
But will taunt relentless
To no avail

For there's a supplicant
Standing
Between two worlds
Calling things that are not
As though they were

Having been admonished
She won't quit
For each victory won
Boasts a new confidence
Commanding
Complete

Lacking nothing in strength
For where she falls short
He supplies the rest
Hold on woman
Don't be weary

Be steadfast

Resistant

And unmovable

The heavens might sway
But they won't move
The waters may recede
The River remains constant

The stars may appear dim
On some certain nights
But the moon is still full
There's no shortage of light

The earth will evolve
On its axles
And some will sit in darkness
Until it returns

Then weeping will give way
To laughter
And those who walked
Among the shadows
Shall receive new life

So she prays
One day into another
The passing of time

The merging of matters
Planting one seed
Gathering the fruit
Of another

Always casting
New bread upon water

I snuggle deep into reticence
Contemplating her journey
Reminiscing

Doris Wellington

The house she built
With sheer faith
Stone upon stone
Words turned miracles
And visited upon
The weak
Made strong
For acts of courage
Incomparable

Mountains
Crumble
Or give way
Pebble by pebble
Until there's
Nothing left
But sand
That the wind gathers
And scatters
To places unknown

Science will record
The mystique of the galaxies
History will note
New discoveries in medicine
Technology accesses the world
With a click of a mouse

But nothing honors God
Like those
Partnered in prayer
To change the cursor of evil

Stalking
An unsuspecting prey
Or pulling from the fire
Those who desire
But can't escape the flames

Declaring the blessings
Of God upon neighbors
Mediating
For those whose voices
Have been silenced

Children
The poor
Widows
Strangers
Babies unborn
Those oppressed
By hatred
And war

She will pray
Until earth yields
Her increase
She may herself stumble
But she will not quit

She guards the future
Holds fast the night
The victory awaits
The daunting task
Of continuance

There is no bread
That hasn't been kneaded
By the leaven that rises
To the challenge

She drinks the cup
Dry, or so it looks
Yet it is full
Supplied to overflow

As her eternal reward
For standing in the gap
With a charge to keep
I spring in action

Open the blinds to life
Pull out the vacuum
There have been visitors
The three-month old carpet
Is a bit soiled
By those who have come

To begin my mission
In the tabernacle
Removing
The dust and dirt of tracking

Back and forth
In the sanctuary
A labor of labor

A mustard seed deposit
For what I know
Will be a generous harvest

July 4, 2012

Some do not believe
That you hear
Or answer my prayers
That we are "religulous"
To a fault

There is no God
Who cares
One way or another
Whether I perish
But the contents
Of my heart
Poured onto these pages
Speaks volumes
To the contrary

Either You speak
Or I am insanely
Mistaken
That somewhere beyond this realm
Of weary toil
And anxious tampering
There is a God
Who hears and responds
To the content
Of a woman's heart

Who not only believes
That you hear me
But that you know me
Intimately
Before I existed
In human body
You knew me
And had known me

Eternally

July 12, 2012

The vine leans forward
Into my window
I reach out to touch it
Then surrender

This is a dream
The bulbs of virgin cotton
Sway across my screen
Undisturbed

I reach for my cell phone
To capture the moment
Fondling the thought
Folding the image into

The recesses of memory
Where I could
When awaken
Download
for further inspection

Why could I not touch it
Caress with soft
Gentle strokes of wonder?

After all

I'm not a stranger to dreams
I walk amongst them as I do reality
The veil has been removed
Access has been granted

What the eyes can't see
In waking
I see through the mystique
Of night vision
Asleep
Yet awake
To a world of possibilities

July 14, 2012

Today I will prove you again
That you honor your word
And respond to prayer
I will take the last of my visible
Finances
And wrap them as gently as I can
In faith

Then sow them
Where I know is fertile soil
Like causes for Israel
Or children who sit alone
Without futures
Widows who eat the bread
Of charity
Or those who need
The light of clarity

It will return in multiplied portions
Pressed down
Shaken together
And running over
It will return in healing for the body
Food for the mind
Doors that revolve
But never close

Hope
And blessings to overflow
The ears will cease to ring
The root cause will be arrested
Strained nerves will relax
And inflammation will vanish

An agent will call
Seeking out the books I birth
From seeds sown in dry seasons
Family will stand
With the offering of forgiveness

Every day will be Sunday
Sabbath shall know no end
General s will plunge their swords
Into plowshares
The lion will lie down with the lamb

My pantry shall never be empty
My pockets shall break from heaviness
The sun will shine through dark clouds

Father they doubt
But I hear you now
The voice is mine

Low

Raspy

But the words are yours
Commanding attention
Drawn from the well
That flow endless

Who but Thee
Can speak with such eloquence
Such unlearned distinction
That crosses the chasm
Of lips teeth and tongue
Bearing the scrolls
Of two worlds

The world is your canvas
With one stroke of genius
You announce your deity
The whole creation
Bows before you
The waters dash against the rock

The wind howls
Against the sea
And she opens wide
The door of her treasures
Exposing the magnificence
Of Her Majesty

July 19, 2012

I am sixty
Three years older than Mudd
When she lost daddy
Eleven years without husband
Or man to caress night yearning

Nowhere to store the excess
Of desire
Except by the tampering of flesh
That leaves the heart dry
Unfulfilled

I am not a manikin
Manipulated
For the eye
Dressed and staged
For window shopping
Alluring to the lust
Of soul
Bereft of substance
And human emotions

Drug and carted off
Between promotions
Discarded when usefulness
Is determined over
I'm not some inanimate object

Turned on for cameras
Clicked off for editing
Valuable only
When others are benefiting

A mere machine
Porous and clogged
From lack of attention
And proper care
Fondled only
For the satisfaction
Of selfish motives

Then stored
In a dark room
Or in plain sight
For public inspection
Or curiosity

Tampering with that
Which is not broken
To flaunt skill
In the presence of apprentice
Who looks on and longs
To know
But has passion to learn
Or skill
Of which to boast

I am a not blank canvas
Not an empty urn
Filled with dead woman's
Ashes
Not fragile glass
To be handled with care
Not a bag of bones
Without sense ability

I am woman
Skin and blood

Woman
Marrow and bone

Woman
Tissue and cartilage

Woman
Sinews and spleen

Woman
Artery and vein

Woman
Prick me and I will bleed

Punch me
And I will swell

Bend me hard enough
I will break

Abuse my labor
And I wane tire
Wear thin of strength
And die
Prematurely

I am woman
Feelings and emotions

Woman
Mind and will

Woman
Break my heart
And it will emote pain

Abandon me to scorn
And I will grieve
Hurt my children
And I will bleed
Endless tears
Of hate and revenge
Deny my rights
And I will blaze
A trail
Of righteous indignation
Upon the pages
Of your history

Disrespect my opinion
And reap the wrath
Of my vengeance
In undeniable success

But I am more than emotions
More than
The intellect of reasoning

Woman
The power of choice

Woman
The will to dream

Woman
The multi-faceted
Multi-tasking

Woman
The creative genius of God

Woman
Building nations
On the backbone
Of faith
And the wings of prayer

Woman
A spiritual force
Made in the image of God

Woman
Created to reign
Woman
Endowed with God purpose
And power
Compassionate and Giving

Woman
Long suffering
And temperate

Woman
Faithful and committed

Woman
Mission minded
And selfless living

Woman
Forgiving and forgetting

Woman
If I disobey
By choices made
I fall from grace

If I live in the sin
Shaped by iniquity
I stagger in darkness

If I rebel against grace
I lose my spiritual center
And fall back
To limited power
I am more than
A lyrical bridge
To a romantic encounter

Or a one-night stand
That leaves the DNA
Of a love child
Worshipped
Or given up for adoption

More than a selected ringtone
That seduces into compromising
Positions
Or abandoned principles

More than the wining and dining
Of indifference
The half-hearted commitment
Of marriage

More than a love note
Tucked under the pillow
To suffice for time
Not given
Or conversation
Not rendered

More than the annual
Valentine
Or Birthday

Giving
That fades a minute after
Midnight

Christmas
And resurfaces
In a New Year's Resolution

"Sorry...

I am more
Than flick date
Or trip to the County Zoo
Bathing in the stench of drained

Satisfying mediocrity
And make do substitutes
For someone who really cares

Father, God

I am Your song
Sung in every language
And in every hue
And tone
Words drafted
From truth

I am the book
Written by Your grace
The front cover
That bear Your name
Author and Finisher
Of my faith

The words flow evenly
Upon the page
Then unevenly they fall
You pick me up
One fragmented phrase
At a time
Then gingerly
You smooth out the edges

Without You
I'm nothing more
Than a dangling participle
A cliché
A metaphor
A euphony
A figure of speech

Inconsequential to context
A farce
Life punctuated
By ambiguities
And exclamation points

OMG!
Over and over again
I stumble
Ensnared again
By the same fault
A run on sentence
Not knowing where to stop

Except for the author's craft

I would be lost
But I'm constantly
Revised
And edited until the content
Reflects
The title of the book

Woman of God
Behold thyself
The Image of God

Born...

Reborn...

July 23, 2012

Father
I saw that sinner again today
The one who sits alone
Body coiled into complacency
Eyes blurred
From too much or not enough
Of something

He flicked the butt of a cigarette
Then rolled a blunt
And passed it to the two buddies
Sitting on his right and left

They sucked in the air
And waved to a woman
Strutting her stuff
In too short jeans
Making her way to them

Her lipstick was smeared
Her lashes curled in despair
Her make-up looked three weeks untouched
And her stomach was exposed
Through the teen halter top

But there was no shame among them
No honor either
Just abstract aloofness
Oblivious to care
Hope abandoned as scorn
Where was it
Who sends
Who's worthy to receive it

Words are clenched between
Rotted teeth
And pa gums
Still she smiled
Wide
And long
Reprobate of care

She had long forsaken
Grief
And gratitude
There were no songs
Being played for her

Only the three comrades
That she met
Every day
Rain or shine
Snow
Or storm
They were one
In misery
And madness
One
Love
Or hate
One penny bag
Or nickel fix
One handout
From a stranger
Lurking along the expressway
Or a busy intercession
Holding up their requests

Homeless
Will work for food

There was no pity between them
No complaints
What one lacked
The other possessed
And shared it
Willingly

There were no complaints
No competition
No questioning
Of loyalty

The sun would rise with them
The weeds spring up
And choke
The heat boil to suffocation
And people gawk
Or toss unkind words
From their windows
Or pathetic stares
While waiting for the light

But their ears are a fortress
Nothing penetrates the emotions
They are past the embarrassment
Way past feeling self-pity

Where there is pity
There is shame
Where there is shame
There is defeat
Where there is defeat
There is no Plan B

So they cast off
The condemnation
Sanity
And reach for the fantasy
It is safer
It will abandon
It will hold steady
Through the night

The rock
Becomes a pillow
The weeds are warm blankets
The litter of the landscape
Is the backdrop
Of a serene portrait
That lulls to sleep

The stench is the savoring
Reminder of life
That death still stalks
But has not apprehended

The drive for tomorrow
To have better luck
Than the day before

The rain is the shield
From heat

The heat is the shield
Of winter

Anything in between
Is a bonus

Where are the children
Who lament their dying
Sinners
Whose only sin is quitting
Giving up the race
Before finished
Future vacated
By excuses
In excess of trying
Rendering the soul
Dead
Because to try
Is to fail

Book 3

Transformed

*What mortal existing by the umbilical cord
of a woman, finite in decaying flesh
Could paint a landscape
on a globally connected canvas of skies
more profoundly magnificent than
the heavens of God?*

I can't even imagine

July 31, 2012

The Giving Tree

Today I stand
Before the giving tree
My spirit lifted
My soul surrendered
My heart overwhelmed

My hands extended
To offer thanks
For what you've already done

Everyday blessings
Left unsung

You've protected me
From danger
Seen and unseen

I know you did Because here I stand
Before the Giving Tree
Unharmed

You've healed my body
Again
Returned it whole

Doris Wellington

I know
Because the feeling
Of moving on empty
Has past
I feel myself again

Delivered
From sin
Committed in ignorance
Or perhaps
Knowledge

Without disobedient intent
Just human
Abstract oblivion
Hitting and missing
Trying and failing
Taking heed
Yet falling
Getting up

Still stumbling

Bumbling

Fumbling

Mumbling

Grumbling

Hold me steady
Lest I slip
Guide my footsteps

Through this
Whatever...
Whenever
I can't articulate why
Or understand

I trust you
Even when
You can't trust me
Giving Tree
Branch of grace
Embrace this twig
This fluttering leaf

Until whole

August 2, 2012

Today the candle I lit for Kenzi
Five days ago
Exploded in liquid wax
The wink succumbed
To the bottom of the jar
I knew that was a sign
That Kenzi was in breakthrough

So at noon today
I lit another
To symbolize
The beginning of new life

The cranberry scent
Of blood red

Liquefied

And I waited for the phone call
To confirm my faith
It came in a text at 1:32

My Baby just opened her eyes
It read
Praise the Lord—Hold on!
I responded

So Maya and I
Locked arms
And danced Hallelujah praises
On Kenzi's behalf

hallelujah
For Jesus
Who partnered with our spoken word
The prayer of agreement
That declares in the present
The thing we desire

We pull from heaven
It is done
Glory
She shall stand on the cirque
Of the earth
And remember

Times spent in heaven
Days in a medical coma
Induced by those
Who promised
But couldn't perform

So they walked away
Assuring the mother
We have done all we know
To do for her

There's nothing left to do
But to make the decision
Should we release her
Back to God

Or wait for God
To give her back to us
He had done it already

She was a preemie
Fighting since the day she appeared
Just a mustard seed
Covered with the afterbirth
Of a miracle

Fragile to the touch
Body swaying like an uncertain
Pendulum
In and out of the hospital

Holding on
Like the champion she is
She must be some kind of prophet

The enemy is back for her again
Doesn't he get it
She's carries the blessings
Of a dual mantle

Apostle and prophet
It's her spirit calling out to us
Here is another opportunity
To watch heaven triumph
Over earth

I see the weak ones
Bobbing and shaking their doubts
In the presence of God...
In the presence of the womb
That bore her here

Let it go

Let her rest

Can't you see her sufferings

But she doesn't agree
The test of will
The will of faith
The temptation to transform
Faithlessness
For those who wait

The test is not hers
It's ours
We are the ones called to believe

While Kenzi lie down
Her will to rest

Until those who know their God
Are convinced
Beyond what we see
Or do not see in flesh

Hold on, little Girl
Time is but fleeting seconds
Flashes of light
Announcing the miracle
We pulled down
From the throne of God

Soon they will be glad
Our faith is stubborn
We have seen the handwriting
Of continuance
The prayer of agreement
That unveils the end
From the beginning

We are not perfect
We are convinced
That God is

So we surrender
The failings
Of human nature
To the Highest Power
Hold on, little Girl
It's just a matter of God

August 5, 2012

The candle of life
Flickered down to the wick
I knew it was time
The call would come
Something has changed

The text came
As sure and testimonial
As the last

My baby moved her hands and feet
She has been moved
From ICU
To general pediatrics

The praise went forth
No holding back
No etiquette
We are the hands and feet
That dance
To Kenzi's song...

August 13, 2012

Eight days ago
We lifted our voices to the sky
Kenzi's alive
Back again
From the citadel of God
Where secrets held
In ancient scrolls
In guarded places
Unknown
Ease the travail
Of a mother's soul

Holding on
Refusing to let go
Every twitch of the nerve
Is regarded a sign
The lift of the brow
The flicker across the cheek
Or the quickening of the hands
Regardless of how fleeting

My child is alive
I shall not relinquish her
She has defied the odds
Held the prudent spellbound
With her tenacious spirit

Physicians with coveted credentials
Specialists in every possible
Aspect of medicine
Held private sessions
Discussing her prognosis
Grim

Impossible to pinpoint her chances

But she will not bow
She will her own doubts

Silent
Against the back splash
Of laughter
And baby talk

She hears in her restless nights
Eyes closed
But not asleep
Body fatigued
But unyielded

Heart bleeding
But still
Consumed by love

Love
That holds captive the dark
Until dawn breaks
Beyond the horizon

Love that quiets
The cacophonies of fear
Until consoled
By the constancy of faith

The substance
Of things hoped for
The evidence
Of things not seen

Mother...

Where is Kenzi
She's where she's been
Since the moment I believed
She's at home
Resting in her baby bed...

Thank You Father,
Once again
For honoring what is yours
The prayer of agreement
The effectual fervent prayers
Of the righteous

The faith...
The operates by love
Yields its harvest
Over
And over

August 14

O magnify the Lord with me
Let us exalt His name together
I will say of the Lord
He is my refuge
My very present help
In the time of trouble

His aim is undaunted
His target is precise
His eye
A piecing arrow
Shoots evil from its watch

The wicked conspires
And crouches at the door
Of the righteous
He lurks with intense secrecy
Waiting for the opportune moment
To strike

He attacks his victims without warning
Then abandons with reckless insanity
There is no turning back to comfort
No thought of the trail of destruction
Or pattern of ruin that follows

What a waste of power
That fails to honor
Or leave a sense of purpose
Beyond here
What an utter loss of being
What an anguish soul that perishes

What hypocrisy
To loyal followers
Who could so easily have the truth
But chooses the lie instead
Celebrating defeat
Prancing and dancing
To the delirium of old wine
When they could have had new

Frolicking in mask
Behind dark
Masquerading as light
Evil sucking the good
Into the inevitability of

An endless night
Vanquished to an abyss
Void of redress
Or exits to another life

Where all are heralded
By the same title
Deceived
Access to the truth

Forever denied
Opportunities to believe

Lost …

While we watch
Our God
Trounce our enemies

He descends upon the wings of eagles
Escorted across the chasm
Of eternity
By legions of known and unknown kind

The feet of gods
Make a path upon the ocean's floor
God walks
There is nowhere to store the excess
The height and breadth
Of all people combined
From every civilization
Since the inception of mankind
Could never rival His statue

And though statue as in spirit
Is generic
Because God is all in all
Existing across the lines
Of distinction
Contained by no definition

Infinitely

September 11

I will come back to the place
To remember
Father I came back to this page
To remember
To set a marker
For those still grieving
Eleven years later
Heart rend beyond mending
Broken by arrows
Shot in darkness
Without warning
For preparation

Children
Torn from the bosom of parents
Orphaned by hatred
That has no repentance
No remorse
For the spewing of venom
Upon the innocent

Who just happen
To live in America

Parents
Lost forever to parenting
One
Two
Entire families
Stolen by malice
That had but one aim

Kill…

It doesn't matter the color
The race
Or ethnicity

Kill…

Whether jew
Gentile
Protestant
Or Catholic
Whether veiled
Or shone
Clothed
Or naked
Whether poor
Or rich
Or basking in wealth

Doris Wellington

Frail
Newly wedded
Or failing in health

Kill...

The babies nursing upon the lap
The student with one semester left
Whether Christian

Muslim
Atheist
Or Skeptic

Black
White
Native or Immigrant

Whether leaving the country
For business or pleasure

There will be no light
At the end of the tunnel

One flickering hope
Consumed by an eternity

The movement of life
Overshadowed

The restless anxiety
Of early morning fatigue
Will not be rested...
In just 33 minutes of chaos
One will be left alone
To grieve another
One will be taken
And the other left behind

Friends will be parted
By strangers
Strangers will become
Forever friends
Children will be abandoned
By default

And parents will be stripped
Of heirs
The world is gripped
By mourning
The morning is gripped
By fear

Faith anchors the soul
As the streets fill
With pandemonium
Bodies are scattered
Across the terrain

Doris Wellington

Swollen by the debris
Of human flesh
Where is God
In all of this
One man says

He does it in the name of Allah
Another says
No loving God
Would permit such a tragic
Useless loss of human life

Before the day has ended
Before names can make the list
Of those missing or feared dead
2900 names will be added

While planes of some
Never arrive

And those who wait for them
Have to hear
They will not...

Where were you Lord?
As babies cried out for parents
And parents searched
Frantically for children

While pregnant women held their bellies
To protect the unborn
And the unborn kicked in protest
As husbands reached out for their wives'
In one last gesture of chivalry
That wouldn't give way to cowardice
Stayed there to die with his wife
The love of his youth
That ring still sparkling
Behind the wealth of smoke
Because the wicked used planes as weapons
Of mass destruction
Heaping their vile convictions
Upon the lives of the innocent

Pledged
To take no prisoners
Where were you Lord?
As veteran stewardesses
And rookie flight attendants

Huddled together in prayer
While assassins walked the aisle
To terrorize their victims

Guiltless

Proud

Unintimidated

Surrendered to death by suicide
Convinced that to die
Was a greater reward
For the evil being rendered

Where were you
When the wicked spiraled out of control
When the blast of bigotry
And hate without restraints
Left the spoils of wrath
Upon the altar of the slain

When the world shared
One tear
Stretched across two great oceans
That could not wash away
The pain
Where were you?

I was there in the cockpit
Bowed between two pilots
Holding the hands of two
Attendants who dared not show their fear
I was there in the 23 Psalms
And the Lord's Prayer
That echoed relentless
Through the atmosphere
As the Holy Spirit lifted
The list of the mourned
Before me

Long before the planes hit
I knew the plan
I stood watch over the air
With 10, 000 legions of soldiers
Armed against evil
Vowed to protect
Those in harm's way

We were not taken by surprise
We were not victims
Not the spoils of a war
We lost
We won

As we do in every threat against good
I was there in the quiet whisper of angels
Leading down long stairwells
And through rubble
That had no fixed path

There

As light in the midst of abject blackness
Eyes in the midst of blinding smoke
Breathing in clogged lungs
And blocked airways

Doris Wellington

There...

In a fresh sip of water
Offered by hands attached to no body
Then disappeared behind singed walls
There in the whimper of a child
Discovered under shrapnel
Just in time

There...

In acts of kindness that bore no name
No ulterior motives
Except
To ease the hurting
Mask the pain
Temporarily
Until some sense was made
Of the calamity

There...
In the bravery of the FDNY

And surrounding counties
As officers of peace
Joined forces
Regardless of rank
Race
Or religion

I was there
In the courage
Of Jeremy Click
And those he convinced to die
With him
As heroes

Knowing death was imminent
Looked evil in the face
And raised the banner of faith
That will live forever
In the pages of history

Remember
The plan was broader than was seen
There were other planes
Plotted to bring national terror
Of epic proportion
Indiscriminately aimed
To take no prisoners

I was there
To foil their harvest
Prove beyond the shadow of doubting

That man plans
But the purpose of God prevails
There were more with us than with them
Much more spirit of travail

Doris Wellington

Many more prayers of the righteous
That intercedes in times of crisis
Many more should have died

But I was there

Infinite power lined the airways
As thousands were snatched
From the grip of death

I hear you asking
How infinite is power
When the loss of one
Was too many?
And those who mourn

Still believe
That the loss of any
Was cruelly senseless

Still…

I was there in the wind
To turn the rudder of the plane
Eastward instead of West
Westward instead of East

Just a mark off course
Made the difference
Between life and death

I snatched the sting of death from souls
The fear of dread
From those who feared

I pierced the smoke with brilliant light
And led soldiers home
On the wings of angels

I was there
Make no mistake about it
Survivals look back
And testify

There was a man at the bottom
Of the stairwell
Calling names
He could not have known
And another
Carrying one upon the shoulder
One by one they came
Rising to the challenge
Surrendering to the cause
All for one
One for all
Where did they get the strength
Where did they get the will
How could they face such odds

I was there…

September 26, 2012

Eight Days in London

Father...
You did it again
I thank you endlessly
My lips swell with praise
And I am silent
No words are transported
Across the chasm
For there are none
So I come to this place
To pour my heart
Onto a blank canvas
Where others will one day read
The way we were

Who would have known
That saying yes
 To an assignment to Rome

Would yield a double harvest
The wayward child came home
Even without me stepping foot
Into that place

And I was granted a ticket
To London
For my birthday
With testimonials
Overflowing with your grace...

Faces light my way with joy
Favor beams like a satellite
Around me
The moment we step on the plane
From Chicago to Heathrow
Testimony swell
To overflow
Step by step
Ordered to perfection
Mind void of understanding
For there were no plans
No itinerary
That included
Such prophetic timing
Such supernatural encounters
Along the way

A young girl at Garrett's popcorn
Hands me a complimentary bag
For accidentally touching my brow
With a stray kernel
Which I pass on to Russ
A pastor between assignments
Seeking his new place

Encouraged
Uplifted
Sent on his way
With prayers and supplications
For a new day

A flight attendant
Flying to London
Overwhelmed by hugs
And smiles from a stranger
Attends to us as though
We were the only passenger
Upon the plane
Though we sat in coach
She extended us first class favor
All the way to our destination

Upon arrival
I slipped her a book
Engraved with thanks
And praise to God
Admonishing her
To keep the faith
There is still a remnant
Whose highest purport
Is to touch the life of those who call

There at Heathrow
The Custom's clerk
Seeing we had no certain address
Hesitated to grant us entrance
Asked what business
We had in London
I simply replied
I'm here for ministry
Where he leads me
I will follow
Down paths to places
I do not know
So, he stamps my visa
And bids me warmly
That his power has granted
Me…move forward

Our phones are dead
We can't make
International calls
So, a young man allows us
The use of his charger
To no avail
Still…
It was honorable

The bags are heavy
We push them forward
As best we can
But there is no strategy
Down the stairs
That leaves us anything
Other than overwhelmed
A British woman sees our struggle
And with white men watching
Takes our luggage
Shaming a man
Who heard our cry

To help these women
Carry their burdens

Doug bravely takes the challenge
An all American
From New York City

Grabs the handle of the biggest bag
And gently steers it
Until we were safe
In the lobby
Of the Grange Holborn
And with conversation that affirmed
His integrity
This might have been my wife's dilemma

And I would hope
That some stranger
Would to my love
Lend his hand

And he was off
And we the more proud
Of our feminine wiles
But greatly appreciative
Of the grace of God

The Grange Holborn surprise me
Her beauty not so much external
But O how beautiful her walls
That held her guest captive
To the opulence of style
And unrivaled service

To room 320 with finesse
And the escort of servants

London...

It had been such a long time
Twenty-two years to be exact
The year of Levi
How could I forget
The love that I surrendered
To fear

Will it be waiting
Could I possibly get a glimpse
Of the one
Who took my heart
And caressed it
To healing
The laughter
Is still piercing
The memories
Stalking to soul
I will not seek him
But if he finds me
As before
I will know
That we are destined
For another chance

But there must be work
Or why am I here
And how will I afford
This five star
Except God has already
Made provision
So I walk as though
He has
I call forth every place and person
That I should stand before
While I'm here

The beauty of the city
Will not captivate me
I'm not mesmerized
By the meandering parks
And cascading gardens
That boost of the monarchy
And prides itself
On the world's greatest
Fish and chips

The River Thames runs along the embankment
Big Ben hovers over
The queen's treasures
The House of Parliament stretches forth its hands
And Buckingham Palace adorns herself
For gawking tourists

Piccadilly Circus
And Oxford streets
Calls the money bearers to come
And traipse the aisles of Harrods
And Regent Street

But I'm impressed but not beyond reason
For I've
Been here
Countless times over

Engorging
What the English take for granted

I walk along cobblestone antiquity
The quaintness of Covent Garden
 And soho

Museums and Cathedrals
Forests and Paths
And neighborhoods of ordinary people

My impression run deep into the vein
Of the unknown

What people see and don't
Or see and don't understand
Of your history

Martyrs
Missionaries
Messages of change
John Wycliff
Martin Luther
Amazing Grace

So I follow the trail
Of the anointed departed
Whose legacy speaks
Through the pages of history

I give books to encourage
Words to lift
Prophesy to direct
Sermons to inspire
Gifts to make the heart happy
Rebuke unto repentance
I lend my presence
To a Jamaica Homegoing
And I am amazed
Of the strength it speaks
To a General laid to rest
From the toils of a
Raging world

Then an African Naming Ceremony
Twins thrust from the loins
Of destiny
Holding on to voices
Prophesying to their future
I join mine with theirs
In the multitude of wisdom
To give birth
In the prayers of agreement

A twenty-year absence
Leaves me with no knowledge
Of what now exists
In the ravaged marriage
Of two friends whom I counseled
To the altar

Dreams woven together
Now a heap of infamy
Looming in the shadow
Of hopelessness
I cannot not fix
So I seek to console the one
And listen with my heart
To what could have been
Prayers are prayed
To lift the veil of the altar
Still spewed with regret
To remove the stain of guilt
And import a new hope
From the bowels of grace
That never fails

A friend languishes
From multiple challenges
Of the body
I make my way to her
In the wee hours of morning
Casting aside
My own weariness
To attend to matters
More urgent than I
This is what I do
This is why I'm sent

To mend the broken hearted
Preach deliverance to captives
And the recovery of sight
To the blind
To set free those who walk in bondage
And to declare
God's acceptable year
Of salvation

A woman leans her spirit
Into my presence
Her hidden desire reaches me
From across the table
Where we sat
Reminiscent
But her anguish soul
Showed no resistance
As I stooped between her
And her friend
To offer both
The prophecy of continuance

My family are all in America
Will you contact them for me
She scribbles numbers upon
Crinkled paper
I slip them into my purse
To convey good intentions

Time moves swiftly
Between the days
There are others
Who will need this ministry

Other reasons that bring me here

A woman
Who looks much like
Any other African American
Leans against a transparent lectern
In Milton Keynes, England
The rolling fields
Of exquisite countryside
Outside of London

We lock eyes
She knows that I am here with purpose
Purpose we both hold
Bound in our loins
One for the other
I am God's
 Authorized representative
To order her steps
Into a new direction
And we concede
To the call of God
In a space
Occupied by those
Who interpret the secret
Of the surrendered

October
In Alexandria

Hurricane Sandy
Forces herself amid
Trepidation
And timidity
The formidable
Builds barricades
To prevent her onslaught
As nature gathers allies
To bolster her power
Water
Wind
Shrapnel
 Gravel
Shingles
Concrete
Trees
And steel
Rallies to her cause

Aligned against human will
There is no match
Evacuate
Or stand in danger of life
Move methodically
Out of her path
Or be carried away
By her wrath

Wrath that bears no identity
No origin of enemy
Or ancestry
Where does all the angry
Come from
And why spew it upon
The lives of the innocent

Driven by pure adrenaline
Gathering the spoil
Of her fury
From the vast ocean
Of warm currents
To the shorelines
Of New Jersey
Snatching away decades
Of history
That has maintained
An industry
Of tourism and trade
Without remission
Now in jeopardy
Of collapse

The aftermath
Speaks volume
To the violent temper
Of a woman scorned

Houses are picked up
And carried to places unknown
Relics and family treasures
Deposited in other people's spaces
Pictures torn from photo albums
Lie face down upon wet soil
Baby shoes
Toys
From Christmases past
And birthday candles

Such small
Mementos
Has no chance to be reunited
With its owner
The wood of pantries
And antique cabinets
Are ripped from iron hing1es
And flung to the uttermost
Place of burial

Grandma bonnet
Is windblown
Three miles down Abbey Lane
And the children
Hold themselves steady
In search of the familiar

Doris Wellington

I am there
I should have been there
But I'm led by what is not seen
As soon as I am hotel safe
The voice tells me
Make a return reservation
Do not linger as planned
Turn your sights
Back to Milwaukee
There's a mighty wind
Rushing up the Eastern Seaboard
Carrying in its bowels
The ravages of nature

Do not be deceived'
Wisdom is your compass
The Spirit your counsel
Move with determined resolve
To be far away
When the rhythm of Sandy
Turns her sight on Virginia
Do not be dismayed
Anchor your hope with obedience

There is no power against
The leading of the Spirit
And so I did
And so it was

As soon as my return flight
Lands
I hear the rumble in the atmosphere
Where eyes does not penetrate
And ears only listen
Thousands of flights are being cancelled
Millions of people
Stumble in darkness
The blunt force of wind
Raptures the waters
And transforms the landscape
To flooding
Climbing to heights
That not even the skilled
Can swim

Faster than First Responders
Can rescue
Mothers trapped in cars
Cars trapped under the trunk of trees
Trees trapped between houses
Houses floating upon waters
Water consuming the landscape
Landscape littered with debris
Debris clogging drains
Drains regurgitating
Vomited sewage
On the pristine innocence
Of Staten Island

Where a barge
Carried by the force of nature
Now rests upon the shorelines
Adjacent to houses
With stunned residents
Watching
With no game plan
To intervene

And I'm safe in the arms of home
Praying for those
Whose less fortunate condition
Is not mine…

November 6—Re-Elected
Voter #904
Father
Is there any precedent
Set for those who serve you
That obligates me to vote
What is my responsibility
As an authorized agent
Of the highest government
Of earthly encounter
Am I required
Is it a sin, or
An affront to humanity
To conscientiously object
To casting my vote this year

I 'm not indifferent to cause
Not at all antipatriotic
Not self-righteous in faith
Or ignorant
Concerning matters of State

I'm a firm believer
That government corals anarchy
And bridges the gap
Between self-destructions
And world disarray
Or itself
Becomes the beast
That devours human prey

The spiritual order of things
Beginning in Eden
Where the law was simply
Man obeying the creator
The surrender of chaos
To the order of nature's
Sublimity

I believe in this America
That it's construct of being
Was Your idea
You were the architect of its highest call

Doris Wellington

You laid the foundation
That fortifies its walls
And its shores
Which became the symbol
Of freedom and democracy

Freedom from the oppressions
Of government
Religion, and
Economic strongholds
Freedom to pursue
Life in its highest form

Free to serve and worship you
The God of our America
Until God became the ideal
Of every man's imagination
And her foundation
Became weaken
By the trampling of other gods

Still I believe
In what you envisioned
A nation that opens her shores
To the wretched
And weary
To raise up a righteous seed
Unto a Holy God

No matter the price she has paid
For her idolatries
Still, she has given birth
To righteous sons
And daughters
From presidents
To paupers
Your name opens the mouths
Of babes and suckling
In a country
Born upon the backbone of religion
The invocation of slaves
Carted from their Mother Country
African
Catholics snatching at rosaries
And purchasing indulges
Lutherans sprinkling grace
Episcopalians vested in
Universality
Methodists catechizing
Universality
Quakers charting the path
Of the Underground Railroad
Shakers
Puritans
Baptists proselytizing through
Baptism
And Holy Rollers
Tongue talkers
Pentecostal
Fanatics

From the Dispensation
Of Human Government
To this present-day contemplation

Can I in good faith
Choose between these two candidates
With an expectation
That one is better suited
To lead this country
When in fact
I've long been persuaded
That the vote I cast
For Christ, my Savior
Superimposes any decision
I make today
For incumbent
Or challenger

I vote because
I'm subject
To the laws
Enacted by those
We elect to follow
I must obey the rule and the exception
Whether I believe or not
Is of no relevance
If I violate in any way
What I have through my vote
Accepted

Or whether I vote or not
The law will hold me liable
Even the scriptures
Admonishes so

So today
Without the slightest reluctance of thought
I order a taxi
I have for six weeks
Been without transport
Except for feet
And the grace of God
That extends beyond
People's motives

As you know, Lord
I'm not registered in Wisconsin
But in Georgia
So I must create the way
To make it happen
It's raining outside
And those responsible for my upkeep
Don't see me
They respond better to themselves

Still...

I must preach and teach
In transparency
The simplest
And purest construct
Of language
That unmasks the hidden
And strips bare
The pretext of carnal wisdom
Revealing
The mind of God
Poured from glorious splendor
Into inglorious vessels

I import
The content of grace given
To baffle the science
Of theoreticians
And theologians
Whose measure of themselves
Amount to a mere grain
Of salt
Without the ability
To transform mortal
Thought
To immortality
Eschatology
Numerology
Tran Substantiation
Predestination

Apologetics
And the politics of religion
So I redirect
To the magnificent
Glorious
That has no construct of form
Except faith
No measure of depth
Except grace
No limitations
Except the psychology
Of indifference
Filtered through the prism
Of fear
No mandate
Except love
No defined destination
Except the heart
Of those who long
The communion of Spirit

To know the impossible
To pierce the veil
Of possibilities
Hidden beyond the analytical
Wall
Of faithlessness
And the confines of science
 Religion
Social order
And the tirade

Of political disorder

To understand the power
And purpose of suffering
Beyond the sainted cause
By which is measured
The fall from human grace
Or to know what
Distinguishes salvation
From what I do today
Or

Is it all the same?

First
I must prove
That I have been a resident here
For at least twenty-eight days
Qualified beyond three years
I search for postal verification
There is none
All mail goes to a PO Box
in a whole different district

The Election Commission
Suggests I use bank statements
So I trudge through cold rain
To obtain what the law requires
To partake in its process

Once obtained
I grab a bite
Of relaxation

Pick up snacks
And Obama cookies
But they're all gone but two
The cookie sheet is still lined
With Mitt Romney's
But he's not my candidate
At least I don't believe so
Standing here
Seeing all his cookies
Staring back at me
Must be some kind of sign
That I'm right

I taxi back
And unload me at home
Then take the two blocks
To the voting poll
Rufus King
International
Baccalaureate High School

The line moves swiftly
As young blacks take their position
In the making of history
When the polls close

either
A Mormon or
A Christian
A Caucasian, or
An African America
Jostling for the highest position
In the world
Will be addressed
"Mr. President"
By his America
But neither is my God

With documents in hand
I register
The decision has since
The cookies
Become clearer
I cast my vote for the incumbent
And placed my "I voted" sticker
Across my chest
Voter #904
Now
It is finished
The rest is up to You
Seven hours Later
Early exit polls indicate
An Obama win

But who can know
There's a seven hour wait
In some cities
To cast a single vote
So, I go to bible study
And prayer
Then back to the television
To watch the returns
An hour or two into the waiting
President Obama
Is officially declared
The winner
The man with the lighted tongue
Wins reelection
He's my president
But not my God

November 22, Thanksgiving

The wind snarls through
Barren trees
The aura of fall
Distinguished by
A prism of colored leaves
Exclusive to Autumn

The allure of nature
Changing her garment
Right before my eyes
Making no apologies
For her nakedness
That is chicly covered by
The reddish-brown
Distinction
Of Thanksgiving trees

Her atmosphere filters
The aromas of Harvest
Through my senses

And I'm thankful for all five
Shoppers walk briskly through markets
Strutting, gliding, tee toddling along
Pitty-pat
 On the trunk of a Maple

Pumpkin, ginger
And vanilla extract
Saturate the nostrils
And turkey
O' the praises would not be complete
Without turkey
Baked
Roasted
Fried
And casseroled
In quiche

There will be no shortage of song
No loss of prayer
As thankful hearts gather
To share the reason for joy

Father I'm saddened by those
Who will spend today in shelters
Because of Hurricane Sandy
Or other natural or human
Travesties
I know the pain of loss
The snatching of life
As one knows it
The sudden removal of the familiar
Without warning

No time to prepare
For anything
Not even the gasp of finality
That renders the vulnerable
Helpless
Homeless
Clinging to Hope
In the face of hopelessness

Still...
There are miracles
To lift up to you
Lives were saved
In spite of pacts made in the dark
By strangers
Banding together for strength

Thank you
For the grace of angels
Who walked along the rift of tides
Slamming against
The New Jersey Shore
Holding back the onslaught
To an even greater degree
Than what was felt

For those who risked their own lives
To save those facing an uncertain death

Thank you for children
Who survived the assault of wind
And water against fragile
Dwellings
While fortresses were toppled
In fatal swoop of nature's breath

Thank you for the generosity
Of neighbors collecting
 The debris of neighbor
Working feverishly to salvage
Any remnant of the life
Being ripped away
Relic by relic

For the uncompromised bravery
Of First Responders
Who live everyday
Under the threat of death
Firefighters
Coastguards
The Red Cross
The Salvation Army
Mayors

Ministers
Police officers
Ordinary citizens

Thank you Father
For ears to hear
The sound of gratitude
Throughout a world
Where the will of people
Test positive
Under every crisis

November 29, 2012

This must be the place
Where God will bless me
Change my name
Manifest my destiny
Current situations
Attest it
Intense difficulties
Protest it

Persecution
False accusations
Lies
Body of flesh
Attacked by inordinate trials

My left arm blistered
With scorching water
Right side neck and back
Under severe
Strained and stretched
To my capacity

I release my cares
For you to carry

Over thinking
Reasoning
Has declared war
On my faculties
I'm still sane
But my conclusions
Are not rational
My judgment clouded
By misperception
I quiet myself

To hear directions

Above the counsel of Rest...

I hear the drum beat of allies
Marching to order
Extending me the comfort
Of a private pity party

The guests list is impressive
I stop to consider it
I can't believe the enemy
Using these giants to enlist me

Eve
Gave Satan a tour of Eden
He pauses temporarily
To enlist her opinion
Makes her feel deceived
By the truth God has given
Feeling deprived of what is good
She desires its rival evil
She pouts about a day
Perhaps a week
Before convincing Adam
Of her decision to eat

Let's do it our way
God is not human
He lives in a bubble
Barking out orders

There's a better way
To obtain forbidden knowledge
Just consume the tree
In the center of the garden
Read her legacy...
Talk to women
Bound by seduction
They can't overcome
Except through Jesus

Compassed about
With such an unusual
Cast of characters
I weigh the benefits
Of adding my signature
To list of warriors
I admire and respect

Moses
Elijah
John the Baptist
Jeremiah
Jonah
Paul, the Apostle

Peter
Solomon
The twelve who scattered
The cripple at Bethesda
Jesus of Nazareth

With that I concede
That to be tempted is no sin
It's the giving up
And not getting up again
So I declined the invitation
The temptation unanswered
Except by reason
Of temporary insanity
Quoting the Infinite
Leaving out infinity
Focusing on the fight
Instead of the victory
Believing the lie
Instead of the truth
Willing to roll over
Calling a truce

Truth be told
The witness themselves declare
They refused the deal
Turned Kingdom's evidence
Laying aside every weight
And besetting sin

They called their witnesses
To the stand
Too
Too much
And Too many More
 Rose to testify
In the presence of God

I'm too forgiven to go back
Too healed to complain
Too much favor to murmur
Too much grace to disdain

Too much mercy to judge
Too many miracles to doubt
Too many promises to forfeit
Too much provision to be without

Too much joy to be sad
Too much life to die
Too many enemies down
Too much courage to cry

Too much faith to fear
Too close to retreat
Too at peace to be confused
Too many victories to seize

Doris Wellington

Too many souls to claim
Too many lives to infect
Too much truth to be deceived
Too much greatness to declare

Too much wisdom to be foolish
Too many witnesses to fail
Too close to turn back
Too many stories to tell

Casting aside any slight
Or rumination
To the contrary
The invitation has merit
Only to those who seek
The ease of fight
Those who want victories
Without enemies
Joy without sorrow
Beauty
Without sack cloth and ashes
Flowers without the withering
Or
Seeds that are trampled
Underfoot by life

There is but one true witness
Ask and it shall be given
Seek and you shall find
Knock and the door shall
Be opened unto

Greatness is pure and simply
Surrender
To the call of God
When and wherever
Seeking daily to imitate
The example of Christ
The greatest
 Of all
Human encounters

Ambition fails
To the limit of self-indulging
Mediocrity
Greatness is a journey
That begins in the mind
For no one is truly great
Who has not sat
At His feet

Suffering brings surrender
Surrender yields
To God inspired
Greatness
All witnesses may step down
The court adjourns
To seek God's Kingdom
And all its righteousness
Until self-fades
To the thunderous backdrop
Of applause

Moses
Elijah
John the Baptist
Jeremiah
Jonah
Paul, the Apostle

Peter
Solomon
The twelve who scattered
The cripple at Bethesda
Jesus of Nazareth

Stands as the prosecutor
Rests his case
We find the defendants
Guilty
Of walking by faith

December 7, 2012

11:24AM

I sit, Father
Life in view
A slideshow passes along the lenses
Of my memory
The glory belongs to you

That I'm still here
Is a story
Laced with hidden challenges
That only you could know

That you alone steered to victory
So only you deserves the glory

Depression swept over me
Like the wind's breath
My soul was silent
No words crossed the chasm
Of tongue

Assaulted by demons
Who thought they'd won
I halted death between
A hatchet and a gun

Abandoned and left for dead
By a husband declaring
Before God I will
Locked out of the house
Where I lived
Keys withheld
By the membership
Twice widowed
Before the age of 50
No children to claim
None to miss me
The bread of provision
Given by the hands of strangers
In the place of solace
And isolation
The language of jesters
Laughing at me in secret codes
The peculiar woman
Who has no invitation
To the celebration of hypocrisy

Look at her...
Her raiment
Is not of the royal sort
For she treads along the path
Of those death to pomp
And the circumcision of fools

She falls and then
Miraculously
Recovers from the snare
Of entrapment

My father's gun
Stalks the night of toil
Why I cry out in anguish
Was I ever born
As if poverty was not enough
I bear the burden
Of a fatherless
Nightmare

Stumbling in and out
Of drunkenness
Sober in seasons
To accommodate
The yoke of family
Wife and children
Gainful employment
And personal responsibility
That forces the innocent
Who depend on your guidance
Into shelters
And inappropriate lifestyles
Seeking what's not in you
They fall for worse
If that's possible

Broken to pieces
Stalked by meager insecurities
That any child should conquer
But can't because
There is no pattern to guide
No principle higher
Except God

So there I am
A child
Chasing the divine
To places I was told You dwell
Only to discover
You were not there
And I stood alone

My child faith
Lifted up to heaven
Where I thought for sure
You were living
Only to discover
You are everywhere
I find myself searching

In the cotton fields of Carolina
The school grounds
Of Darden
The walks along Pender Street
To the library
Where pecans trees
Will temporary
Answer hunger

In the choir stand
Of Piney Grove
Where my mother wailed
For the same reasons I did
Shed tears upon the floor
Of the altar
Invoking out loud
To the silence

Only to discover you
In the bathroom
Bent over in sorrow
Head butting the darkness
Not allowing me to falter
Among eyes
That watched for my fall

How many times
Have my heart been broken
And then put back together
To show me
That you were there
Even in pain and suffering

Revealing the construct
Of Destiny
In places
And circumstances
Rejected by those
Who seek the science of knowing

There in the slighted detour
Away from purpose
Whether planned
Or accidental
Constant

You were there
When a crazed
Would be rapist
Spoke seductive whispers
Under the influence
Of cocaine
Trying to force himself
Passed the walled place
Of virginity

Never considering
That I was a warrior daughter
Who dared to fight
Until he abandoned his arms
And surrendered to the force
Of determination
Father
Your eyes have always followed me
Always marked
The places of my naivety
Choosing to see the best
I've danced
Unknowingly with evil
But you found me
In fetal position
Wrapped in sack cloth
And ashes
Stumbling along the path
Of the surreal

I stumble over a jiggered
Rock
And twisted my ankle
Refusing crutches
 I wore
A soft casket
To correct the sprain

All while crushed
By unfulfilled promises
Heart swinging like a
Broken pendulum
That waits for a man
To repair the breach
But there is none
No one ever comes
Except...
You

Three years later
The word of knowledge
Warning me
Against the impending
Force of gravity
I fell sidelong
Onto the pavement
From a moving bike

Compromising my strength
Six months still mending
I suffered a hairline fracture
On the same side
Dancing for a victory
That wasn't quite
Secure

But you stayed my sanity
Even when the fire came
To destroy things written
Over years of inclining
To the voice of the Spirit
The legal document
Suffered smoke damage
But the vision
Remained intact

And while the greedy
Carted away the material
Tangibles
And the sheriff
Enforced the eviction
Of property

Church folk
Came deliberately
To ransack
The spoils of war
And all was lost
Except
Studies in prayer
Hidden from the eyes
Of those
Who stumble in the dark

Then one harvest
They came for me
Wrapped in the deception of food
Chocolate covered peanuts
That hid my fatigue
And comforted my weariness
Eat them all
To the delight
Of soul
There is no better respite
Than the food of pleasure
Across the pallet
Of indifference
As each bite
Is savored to indigestion

As the dusk folded into darkness
And the body drained
Surrendered to the force of
Haste and anxiety
Stress and strain
Compromised rest
The taunting of pain
The body speaks
From places unknown
 You feel the rippling of disquiet
But cannot touch
The place
From which it springs

Then...
Precipitously
A performance
Convulses the entire being
Threatening
To the core of calm
That you cannot arrest
Not even with prayer
And song
The body is at the center
Of a crisis
You cannot breathe
The heaviness presses inward
But does not relent
One sister rebukes the devil
The other pulls over
And calls EMS

For four months
The body wrestles
Against the unknown
No diagnosis
Concedes to ignorance
What is it
And from where did it come

A different sister
Same DNA
Makes a startling claim

"I saw the witches
Trying to assay your strength
Attempting to strip
You of your garment
And put you in theirs

But you would not give over
Your determined resolve
More forceful
Than they
The army that held you
More powerful in faith
They attacked
 To no avail
Every cunning
Strategy failed
And there I was
Caught up
With God
Safe…
Sound…
Indomitable force

The Heavens Trembled
12-12-12

The heaven shook with thunder
Past the midnight
Of a new beginning
That comes and goes
Only once in one hundred
There must be words
That could not have been spoken
Secrets that could not
Have been revealed
Until the moment of this
Portal
When the windows of heaven
Open
And thundered the will
Of years
Wrapped in the loins
Of the Father

Millions hoped in opaqueness
Waiting to glimpse
Perhaps even embrace
The appearance of the twelve
That brings with it
The end
And the beginning of things

Doris Wellington

Tearing down the old
Building the new
Establishing that which will
Forever remain

Ignorance obscures
The power of the veiled
There is no way to understand
The divineness
Of the 12
In which God
The Sovereign
Inaugurates Himself
In systems
And codes

That governs
Earth and heaven

Marking the places
Where they meet
The balancing of power
The keeper of those who sleep

12 divisions of heaven
Open
And out of them
God speaks

Daughter
"You've entered your latter rain
You must not be afraid...

The prayer that triples
Indemnity
Remuneration
Guaranteed compensation
For services rendered
Annuity
Now compounded
And capitalized
Over years of sowing
Your seed

The increase
Unstoppable
It's time
To rule and reign
In the abundance
Of your dream

I know you've heard
Rehearsed
Reworded it
Confessed it over
To a million refrains
Until the lyrics have become
Monotonous
The expectation
Still delayed

But today
Yes...
Sweet today
Twelve past midnight
August 12
In the year of our Lord
Two-thousand twelve
The heavens
Thundered
No longer than 12 seconds
With the sound
That pierced the void

This is the day
Of a new beginning
What had not been seen
Or heretofore hidden
Has now been established
On earth
From heaven

And all the daughters
In waiting
Rejoice
This is the Day
And promise
Of our Lord

Shaking all
That can be shaken
And firmly planting
All that remains

I believe...
Understanding
Is not necessary
At this stage
It will come
When needed
Speak
In necessity
Declare itself
Above any doubting

Heaven has spoken
Earth has received
The bequeath
Of promises
For latter rain
Years removed
From this page
Testimonies
Shall rise and speak
To the inexorable harvest
Of the latter rain.

I Surrender

December 14, 2012
Newtown, Ct

Grief washed over me
Like rain
Relentless grief
Rapidly taking the shape of anger
There is no reason
Twenty children bequeath
By God
Should be so soon
Snatched away
With six guardians
Who rose
Embracing the day
With expectation

No reason to suspect
That before the day
Ended
Newtown would lose
It's innocence
The virgin
Serenity
Of an entire community
Shifting emotions
Between grief
And guilt

Anger and anxieties
That nothing academic
Could fix

No amount of privilege
Or preconceived security
Would ever fill the void
Of twenty
Murdered children
At the hands of one
Who was no stranger
A friendly smile
Familiar body language
No need to worry
He bore the breath
Of the First Adam
He had been there before
There was no threat
To consider
No danger to avoid

No reason to suspect
Unlike any other day
That life at Sandy Hook
Would never be the same
There is however the prayer
A new town will emerge
From out of the darkness
A beacon of Love

Understanding fails
Where is the grace
That sleeps
While evil lurks
And men of conscious
Fatten themselves
With the food of comfort
Sightless
To the world of pain
Excusing themselves
It's not my place
To confront the devil
Let him reign

I have no power
No will or purpose
No desire
To intervene
In the despair
Of humans
Even when
Those most vulnerable
Are our children

Where are the mediators
Between good and evil
They're few
And far between

The world turns on
The axle of fear
Every face is a stranger
Rather than
A human being

The same DNA
Marks us all
It doesn't matter
From where we come
We cannot get there
Being afraid
The universe cringes
Where cowards tread
Upon the souls
Of children

Innocence stolen
Brilliance buried
Obituaries
And
Epitaphs too soon
Prepared

Yes, we say
God has called them
Upward
To a better place

This is the solace
That consumes our grief
Until the night subsides
And life continues
Without their faces

Their footsteps
Silenced by an insanity
We can't erase
Wings clipped too soon
By lascivious greed
Sexual predators
Serial killers
That have no regard
Of age
Preying on the weakest
Victims
Who too deserves
The right to life
Without the envies of death
Hovering over their days

Where are the valiant
Those sent
To intervene
Interact
Interfere
Interpose themselves
Between
Life and death

No special talents
No resume
No professional skills
Nor Ph.D.
Just the pure
And simple call
The force of purpose
The love of God
The will to change
Time to share
The mantle of Elijah
The faith of Sarah

The yielding of Samuel
The courage of Esther
The spirit and sacrifice
Of John the Baptist

Fearless
Unintimidated by evil
Walking surreally
On the edge of living
Everyday seeking to engorge
The task
That cowards avoid
Waking to the challenge
Breathing for the chance
The heartbeat of destiny
The life blood of change

Are you one of them
I am...

Newtown
I feel your pain
I light a candle in your dark
To pierce your night
With my heart
Hear me
Wherever you are

Charlotte
Daniel
Rachel
Olivia
Ana
Josephine
Dawn
Dylan

Madeleine
Mary
Jesse
Chase

Allison
Emilie
Jessica
Grace

James
And Jack
Anne Marie
Noah
Caroline
Catherine
Benjamin

Lauren
Allison
Victoria
Avielle

Vindication
December 15

I saw Lucifer fall
Like lightning
Without umbrella
To shield
From the latter reign
From heaven down
Into hell

Still stumbling
Now Satan in full
Without redemption

Fully compensated
For the evil he rained
Selling tickets
To destruction
Heartache
And Shame

Suicide
Fornication
Sadistic greed
Lying for no reason
Except to deceive

Inordinate desires
Perverse intentions
Racist Hatred
Murder of children

Making promises
That will not secure
The future
Granting one way access
To an endless tunnel

Nowhere to run
Nowhere to hide
No covering for those
Wooed and beguiled

The end of faith
Invested in negative results
The wages of sin
The reward for believing for naught

December 20

26 Acts of Kindness: One Prayer of Repentance

December 21

We have crossed the chasm
To a new anointing
The body of Christ
 Her great warriors
Standing on the cirque of time
Aligning with the government
Of God

Generals to the front
Without the thought to fail
Shaking down the powers of darkness
Bombarding the atmosphere
Tactical
Strategic
And unafraid
Manifest the mandates of God
For which creation waits

With the Holy Spirit
Leading the assignment
Caves will be emptied
Of prophets in hiding

New sound
New voices
New music from heaven
Hypocrisy will be shattered
By the spirit of humility

Apostles
Will be identified
According to Apostolic
Ascendency
All ages
Nationalities
Identifying one another

Male and female
One connected assignment
Shall carry in their loins
Divine authority and power
The revelation of things
Heretofore hidden
Will overtake the doctrine
Of manmade traditions
There shall be a great shaking
In the realm of heaven
False teachers and prophets
Shall be exposed by numbers

True Apostles will emerge
From the most unusual places
Carrying a word
That shall convert entire nations
Heads of nations
Are being released in agreement
Within twelve months
Twelve will convert
 To Christianity

The urgency
And expediency
Of things to come
Will gather the scattered remnant
And make them one

From every profession
And walk of life
Protestant and Catholic
Jew and Gentile

Male and female
From ages across years
From religious
Wandering
They shall appear

Carrying the book
And horn of the Lord
Purged
And positioned
In righteous adorn

Ready to slay
The abominations
Of the wicked
Lies that bound truth

Confusion
That interrupts peace
And the rancor
Of alarms

The world will not end
By the mouth of the false
But according to the promise
In the word of the Lord
This is the day
The trumpet will sound
To break the wall of resistance
Of those who defile
The temples of God

Let your feast days continue
Be fat with drunken blindness
Stumble and stagger
                              In your vile
While vultures
Consume your madness

Wallow in the vomit of dogs
The days of your reveling
Are numbered
But not today
The world shall not end
You 're not that cunning

Let those who imagine
Your vanities
Be driven
 By your practice
You spew your bowels
Upon the weak
Then laugh
At their famish
So hug your world
With lamentations
Burst forth in derision
Cast your own soul downward
For you have long been finished

As for me...
My life is just beginning
A word is knocking at my door
I must rise
And walk in my surrender
I am one of those released
To stand
So the world cannot be ending
There remain dreams
Innumerable
And promises
I must mentor

My voice has been released
To nations
There is no time
For weeping
No time to celebrate
Or regret
What did or did not happen

December 27
The Wedding Gown Speaks
"Prepare to be a Bride"

The wedding gown
Pranced before me
Gathering the voice
Of wedding dreams gone by
The sand dust of fine gold
Illuminated the ballroom
Until the whole night
Was filled with her song

I am your wedded bliss
You are my bride
The time has come
To fulfill your desire

Adorn your solace
With laughter
Cover your widowhood
With song
 Release your heart
To love reborn

Waltz with me
Through the corridor
Where a thousand ballerinas
Await your call
Arise to the moment
Embrace the tempo
Know that your time
Has come

Your groom overflows
With ballads
To serenade the wife
He longs
Nothing can keep
Him from you
The heart yearns
And races to fulfill
Its hunger

Favorable years overtake
Your days
The cold has turned to warmth
Wounds heal

Pain gives way
To joy
Do not tell me
I cannot love
I love because I can
And now love stands before me
Knocking
Once again

As the night flees
Before me
A celebration of angels
Hailed
"Daughter, I crown you worthy
And ready
 To wear the veil

Cast off the yoke
Of loneliness
Draw from the
Promise Well
Arise...
The King stands guard
To honor your travail

Dance
With seraphim watching
Sing until they joins with us

Happiness
Consumes desolation
The womb is now
With child

There are no eyes
That do not see
No ears
That have not heard
No heart
That does not feel
The passion of your love

December 31, 2012
12-13-2012

The year comes to a swift halt
But it holds a hidden promise
Read the date as it stands
You're see the increase coming

Not another moment
Beyond midnight
I pause
To offer a prayer
I bow
On synthetic carpet
At my sister's house

And I thank God
There was no reason
To ask
I was not a supplicant
I was a giver of thanks
For things done
I can no longer
Remember
And miracles
That still hover
In the atmosphere

My Lord.
My God
How great
How glorious
And magnificent
If I had a million tongues
I would still miss something
There would be some
Element
Of my testimony
That is left unsaid

There is simply no way
To put in words
All what you have done
Danger
Seen
And unseen
Prayers thought
Not spoken
Gifts and surprises
Prayers answered
Healings
And deliverances
At a word

Financial miracles
Like Rome
And London
Without preparation
Or money

How do you do it
God...
How do you do it

Command the universe
With a nod
Leave your throne
And back
Before heaven knows
You're gone
In a split second
Responding to
Children
Threatened by
Satan's scorn

You snatched
A ten-month Kenzi
From a coma
And reversed the edict
Of hospice
For Precious Thomas

You continue to heal mom
Destroying every threat
Against her promise
She honored her father and mother
Her days should be long

She taught me how to pray
She presented me to you
Gave us reason to live
And not die
Showed us
The other side
Of possibilities

How do you do it?
Lord
How?

Deliver me from evil
Beat back the threat
Of weariness
And the challenge
Of test and trials
Keep me singing
Praising
Even when I'm tired

I find myself
Muttering
Proclaiming your word
Be not weary in well doing
You shall reap in due season
If you faint not

Here
On the threshold of tomorrow
You've done again
2012 has passed
As a story lived
And here I am
Surrendered
Waiting the unveiling
Of another year

Another 365 Days
To experience you like never before

Prayer for Salvation

If you desire a relationship with the Lord and you believe that it is possible; read and follow the instructions of Romans 10:9-10 or contact someone who is living a sincere experience in Christ and ask that person to walk you through the scriptures and pray the prayer of salvation with you. When the heart is sincere, accepting Christ as your Savior is just as simple as the scriptures have made it.

Doris Wellington

Former American University student and North Carolina native; Doris Wellington, is an ordained minister, spiritual life teacher, public speaker, dream analyst, and visionary writer.

She has effectively interwoven and branded a wide range of products, services and innovative ideas that bridge the power and potential of spirit, soul, and body. "Without this triumphant interaction, we would never understand, nor could we ever apply the full range of our God-given abilities." Recognizing that the grace of our gifts comes from God, **Doris Wellington** delivers life changing spiritual, motivational, and educational conferences, media, theatre, and visionary business concepts and creative ideas.

She has authored, twenty epic stage plays, including the celebrated allegorical production, *I Waltzed with God the Morning of Genesis: A Mosaic for Peace,, Dead Woman Dancing on Her Grave, and God, I'm Here and I'm Colored: the National Debate on Race and Equality.* She is the author of the thirteen-book poetic epistolary, *Romancing God: The Divine Love Affair;* as well as The Divine Notebook: Letters and The Poverty Manifesto.

Additionally, she has authored four novels, and one memoir, The River God Runs through Her. She coauthored Stokestown: Dreaming behind Closed Doors., 2015. She has recorded and studied more than 20 000 prophetic dreams, visions, and supernatural visitations. She founded and wrote the curriculum for **The Prophetic Path Dream Summit***, which teaches the prophetically inclined how to tap into the hidden power of dreams.*

Doris Wellington travels internationally as a minister and motivational speaker.

Dwelling Places
Home of Books and Letters
By Doris Wellington

Amazon.com, Createspace.com, BarnesandNoble.com

The River God Runs through Her: Praise for an unlikely Champion
Stokestown: Dreaming behind Closed Doors
Romancing God: the Divine Love Affair Volumes Series
Pastoral Letters: the Essential Collection
Collateral Damage: The Anatomy of Effective Prayer
Passover Ponderings: Meditations From Lent to Pentecost
Tell Me Your Truth, I'll Sell You My Lie: Behind the Veil of Santa Claus
The Offering of Stone Leadership Sabbatical
Winter's Dark, A Love Story
Behind Enemy Lines: Strategist Weapons of Spiritual Warfare
The Dear John Reader: Rituals of Disclosure in Love
and Emotional Emancipation
Dead Woman Dancing on Her Grave
Woman in a Jar: Narratives of a Perfect Insanity
Breakthrough Worship
Angela of Gods: A Sister's Tribute To An Unsung Activist
God, I'm Here and I'm Colored: the National Debate on Race & Equality
The Hurt Café: How to Have a Breakdown without Going Crazy
Tour of the Apostle: A Memoir of Days Tribute to My Mother

www.ingramcontent.com/pod-product-compliance
Lightning Source LLC
Chambersburg PA
CBHW052043220426
43663CB00012B/2427